PERSPECTIVES
ON MARRIAGE

ACTA
ASSISTING CHRISTIANS TO ACT
PUBLICATIONS

Perspectives on Marriage is designed to be used in a formal program of marriage preparation, although it can also be useful for an individual couple working on their own. A Leader's Guide to *Perspectives on Marriage*, which contains various program formats for marriage preparation, is also available from ACTA Publications.

Revised by Leif Kehrwald
Edited by Gregory F. Augustine Pierce
Cover design by Tom A. Wright
Typesetting by Garrison Publications

We wish to express our gratitude to Ms. Elizabeth Bannon, Ms. Patricia Dondanville Berman, Ms. Mary Buckley, Rev. Thomas Hickey, Rev. Gerald Joyce, Mr. Chris Malone, Rev. Daniel Polizzi, Ms. Karen Skerrett, Mr. William Urbine and Mr. Daniel Wyatt, as well as numerous family life ministers, for their generous contributions of time, expertise and experience in the preparation of this booklet.

Excerpts from the English translation of Rite of Marriage © 1970 by the International Committee on English in the Liturgy, Inc. are used with permission. All rights are reserved.

ISBN: 0-915388-34-0

01 00 99 98   10 9 8 7 6 5 4 3 2

Printed in the United States of America

CONTENTS

Instructions 4

Exercises on Communication

How Do You See Me? .... 5 and 7

Clue Each Other In .... 6 and 8

Discovering Each Other .... 29 and 31

Please Listen to Me 40

Our Favorite Things .... 69 and 71

Exercises on Conflict Resolution

Fighting Fair 9

Fighting without Fighting 10

On Our Worst Behavior .... 11 and 13

Try, Try Again .... 12 and 14

Exercises on Families of Origin

Where We Come From .... 17 and 19

My/Your/Our Family .... 18 and 20

Exercises on Hopes and Dreams

Great Expectations .... 21 and 23

Read the Future .... 70 and 72

Exercises on Intimacy

Toward Intimacy .... 25 and 27

Intimacy Checkup .... 26 and 28

Sex and Sexuality .... 65 and 67

Exercises on Explosive Issues

The Bells Are Ringing 15

Play Solomon 33

Take This Job .... 45 and 47

Beat the Clock .... 46 and 48

Alcohol and Drugs .... 49 and 51

Look before You Leap 63

Living Together 77

Domestic Abuse 78

Exercises on Religious Faith

Sharing the Faith Vision .... 35 and 37

Two Faiths, One Love 39

Living the Sacrament 79

Exercises on Planning a Family

Now's the Time .... 41 and 43

Are We Ready? .... 42 and 44

Remarriage .... 73 and 75

(Step)Fathering and (Step)Mothering .... 74 and 76

Exercises on Money Matters

The Dollar Almighty? 53

Your Financial House 54

Knowing the Territory .... 55 and 57

NUDEL .... 59 and 62

Your First Year Budget 60

Your decision to marry—to commit yourselves to one another forever—may well be the most important decision you have made, or will make, in your lives. Learning how to communicate effectively with each other is at the heart of marriage and therefore should be central to your marriage preparation. So don't spend all of your time before the wedding planning the reception, designing the rings, or furnishing your new home. Spend some time on your relationship.

This workbook is designed to help you take a good, long look at marriage. Not just *any* marriage, but *your* upcoming marriage

Perspectives on Marriage contains thought-provoking exercises to help you think through and share your thoughts and feelings about marriage, its meaning and its challenges. Don't merely fill out and exchange the exercises. Their value occurs *after* the exchange, when you begin to probe, share feelings, question, and work to understand each other more deeply. The exercises are tools designed to:

- promote and stimulate dialogue
- deepen mutual understanding
- elicit insights and feelings

about potentially sensitive areas that might not otherwise be discussed.

In some of the exercises, two copies are provided so that each of you can complete one individually and then discuss your responses together. Other pages contain "discussion starters" for you to read and think about together.

The value of these exercises is in the dialogue they provoke.

HOW DO YOU SEE ME?

You are invited to compare your views of yourself with your fiancée's view of you. This exercise emphasizes the fact that the image we have of ourselves is not necessarily the image that even those near and dear to us have.

A. MAN ABOUT HIMSELF

	VERY	SOMEWHAT	NEUTRAL	SOMEWHAT	VERY	
calm	__	__	__	__	__	excitable
assertive	__	__	__	__	__	passive
reserved	__	__	__	__	__	affectionate
skeptical	__	__	__	__	__	trusting
extroverted	__	__	__	__	__	introverted
self-questioning	__	__	__	__	__	confident
procrastinating	__	__	__	__	__	compulsive
spendthrift	__	__	__	__	__	tightwad
happy-go-lucky	__	__	__	__	__	careful planner
realist	__	__	__	__	__	optimist
detached	__	__	__	__	__	sympathetic
social	__	__	__	__	__	private
serious	__	__	__	__	__	whimsical
relaxed	__	__	__	__	__	intense
critical	__	__	__	__	__	permissive
liberal	__	__	__	__	__	conservative
uncommunicative	__	__	__	__	__	communicative
self-sufficient	__	__	__	__	__	reliant
open	__	__	__	__	__	reticent
organized	__	__	__	__	__	disorganized
practical	__	__	__	__	__	dreamer
cautious	__	__	__	__	__	bold

B. MAN ABOUT WOMAN

	VERY	SOMEWHAT	NEUTRAL	SOMEWHAT	VERY	
calm	__	__	__	__	__	excitable
assertive	__	__	__	__	__	passive
reserved	__	__	__	__	__	affectionate
skeptical	__	__	__	__	__	trusting
extroverted	__	__	__	__	__	introverted
self-questioning	__	__	__	__	__	confident
procrastinating	__	__	__	__	__	compulsive
spendthrift	__	__	__	__	__	tightwad
happy-go-lucky	__	__	__	__	__	careful planner
realist	__	__	__	__	__	optimist
detached	__	__	__	__	__	sympathetic
social	__	__	__	__	__	private
serious	__	__	__	__	__	whimsical
relaxed	__	__	__	__	__	intense
critical	__	__	__	__	__	permissive
liberal	__	__	__	__	__	conservative
uncommunicative	__	__	__	__	__	communicative
self-sufficient	__	__	__	__	__	reliant
open	__	__	__	__	__	reticent
organized	__	__	__	__	__	disorganized
practical	__	__	__	__	__	dreamer
cautious	__	__	__	__	__	bold

Mark list A about yourself by checking one, *and only one*, of the five lines between each set words above: (each of the lines is keyed to one of the words above: very, somewhat, neutral, etc.). Check one line you feel most nearly describes your personality, e.g., in the first set of words it might be "very excitable" or "somewhat calm." Then proceed to the next set of words.

Next, mark list B about your *fiancée* by checking the line that most nearly describe your partner's personality traits for each set of words.

Compare your sheet with your partner's by holding them side by side. First compare A and D, then compare B and C. Discuss the differences in your perceptions of each other.

CLUE EACH OTHER IN

Your beloved has traits, qualities, and ways of acting which you especially prize and appreciate, which you wish he or she would develop even more. *But your partner is not a mind reader.* Tell him or her those qualities you find especially attractive. Most certainly love will lead your partner to concentrate on them even more.

Read the qualities presented (to the right). Pick out and list the seven you appreciate most in your partner. Feel free to include other qualities not on our list—these might be the most important of all. Next to each quality, write down one recent example of how your beloved demonstrated that quality.

Flexible and open
Imaginative
Socially at ease
Cares about people
Considerate of others
Confident and secure
Understanding
Hardworking
Cares about a home
Affectionate
Sexually attractive
Even-tempered
Patient with me
Strong
Gentle and kind
Makes me laugh
Interesting and alive
Accepting and tolerant
Dependable
Talks to me
Compromising
Intelligent
Listens to me
Spiritual
Turns me on physically

What I appreciate about you most is: A recent example:

1. _____   _____

2. _____   _____

3. _____   _____

4. _____   _____

5. _____   _____

6. _____   _____

7. _____   _____

HOW DO YOU SEE ME?

You are invited to compare your views of yourself with your fiancé's view of you. This exercise emphasizes the fact that the image we have of ourselves is not necessarily the image that even those near and dear to us have.

C. WOMAN ABOUT HERSELF

	VERY	SOMEWHAT	NEUTRAL	SOMEWHAT	VERY	
calm	__	__	__	__	__	excitable
assertive	__	__	__	__	__	passive
reserved	__	__	__	__	__	affectionate
skeptical	__	__	__	__	__	trusting
extroverted	__	__	__	__	__	introverted
self-questioning	__	__	__	__	__	confident
procrastinating	__	__	__	__	__	compulsive
spendthrift	__	__	__	__	__	tightwad
happy-go-lucky	__	__	__	__	__	careful planner
realist	__	__	__	__	__	optimist
detached	__	__	__	__	__	sympathetic
social	__	__	__	__	__	private
serious	__	__	__	__	__	whimsical
relaxed	__	__	__	__	__	intense
critical	__	__	__	__	__	permissive
liberal	__	__	__	__	__	conservative
uncommunicative	__	__	__	__	__	communicative
self-sufficient	__	__	__	__	__	reliant
open	__	__	__	__	__	reticent
organized	__	__	__	__	__	disorganized
practical	__	__	__	__	__	dreamer
cautious	__	__	__	__	__	bold

D. WOMAN ABOUT MAN

	VERY	SOMEWHAT	NEUTRAL	SOMEWHAT	VERY	
calm	__	__	__	__	__	excitable
assertive	__	__	__	__	__	passive
reserved	__	__	__	__	__	affectionate
skeptical	__	__	__	__	__	trusting
extroverted	__	__	__	__	__	introverted
self-questioning	__	__	__	__	__	confident
procrastinating	__	__	__	__	__	compulsive
spendthrift	__	__	__	__	__	tightwad
happy-go-lucky	__	__	__	__	__	careful planner
realist	__	__	__	__	__	optimist
detached	__	__	__	__	__	sympathetic
social	__	__	__	__	__	private
serious	__	__	__	__	__	whimsical
relaxed	__	__	__	__	__	intense
critical	__	__	__	__	__	permissive
liberal	__	__	__	__	__	conservative
uncommunicative	__	__	__	__	__	communicative
self-sufficient	__	__	__	__	__	reliant
open	__	__	__	__	__	reticent
organized	__	__	__	__	__	disorganized
practical	__	__	__	__	__	dreamer
cautious	__	__	__	__	__	bold

Mark list C about yourself by checking one, *and only one*, of the five lines between each set words above: (each of the lines is keyed to one of the words above: very, somewhat, neutral, etc.). Check one line you feel most nearly describes your personality, e.g., in the first set of words it might be "very excitable" or "somewhat calm." Then proceed to the next set of words.

Next, mark list D about your *fiancé* by checking the line that most nearly describe your partner's personality traits for each set of words.

Compare your sheet with your partner's by holding them side by side. First compare A and D, then compare B and C. Discuss the differences in your perceptions of each other.

CLUE EACH OTHER IN

Your beloved has traits, qualities, and ways of acting which you especially prize and appreciate, which you wish he or she would develop even more. *But your partner is not a mind reader.* Tell him or her those qualities you find especially attractive. Most certainly love will lead your partner to concentrate on them even more.

Read the qualities presented (to the right). Pick out and list the seven you appreciate most in your partner. Feel free to include other qualities not on our list—these might be the most important of all. Next to each quality, write down one recent example of how your beloved demonstrated that quality.

Flexible and open
Imaginative
Socially at ease
Cares about people
Considerate of others
Confident and secure
Understanding
Hardworking
Cares about a home
Affectionate
Sexually attractive
Even-tempered
Patient with me
Strong
Gentle and kind
Makes me laugh
Interesting and alive
Accepting and tolerant
Dependable
Talks to me
Compromising
Intelligent
Listens to me
Spiritual
Turns me on physically

What I appreciate about you most is: A recent example:

1. _____   _____

2. _____   _____

3. _____   _____

4. _____   _____

5. _____   _____

6. _____   _____

7. _____   _____

Take a moment to recall a recent conflict between you and your partner. Perhaps it was just a small misunderstanding, or maybe something major. What were the circumstances of the problem? Replay the event in your mind. How was the issue resolved? Have the two of you reconciled? How did you feel once the two of your had reconciled?

Someone once said that if you want to avoid conflict you will have to forego all intimacy. Not for us, thanks! Conflict is a part of every close relationship. The more intimate we are, the more vulnerable to hurt we become. As the two of you grow closer in love, you also become more aware of your differences in such things as assumptions and expectations of each other, abilities to listen, family backgrounds, communication patterns, habits, etc. Sometimes, the very things that attracted the two of you to each other in the beginning become the characteristics that grate and cause conflict later on.

To presume that you will never argue is too idealistic and simply not true. Yet working through a "good" conflict can be healthy for your marriage because it usually brings issues to the surface and clears the air between you. Remember, the flip side of conflict is intimacy. There are positive ways to handle conflict and "fight fair." The "DOs & DON'Ts" on the right can help you avoid the destructive and disheartening potential of marital conflict.

DO

1. Give each other equal opportunity to speak
2. Stick to the issues at hand.
3. Complete the argument. Come to some resolution, even if it means setting a later time to do so.
4. Seek first to understand the other, then to be understood.
5. Admit when you are wrong. Graciously accept the other's admission of guilt or wrong-doing.
6. Make up and mean it.
7. Call forth the core love you have in your heart for each other. Remember the vow you made to make your marriage work.

DON'T

1. Dominate the argument.
2. Dredge up past hurts or problems, whether real or perceived.
3. Postpone a resolution indefinitely.
4. Sling mud and arrows. Avoid put-downs, yelling and name calling. Terms such as "stupid jerk," "fat slob," "drunken bum," or "airhead" only incite more anger and hurt.
5. Use physical violence...ever!
6. Use sex as a source of power or manipulation. Never threaten to withdraw love or sex.
7. Use the "silent treatment."
8. Always give in. Your resentment will build because the conflict hasn't really been resolved.
9. Make a scene. Never deliberately embarrass each other in front of others. Most conflicts need private space and time to be resolved.

While an argument may have its benefits in the long run, it's not exactly a pleasant experience—and it's certainly not what you are getting married to do. First of all, some things are just not worth arguing about. Remember, it's "for better or worse." You also need to learn now—before the wedding—the difference between the "negotiables" and the "non-negotiables" for both you...and your partner.

Still, there will be plenty of serious issues in the years ahead that will produce conflict. You both must stand up for what you believe and express your expectations. But you must also be willing to grow and change. Most conflicts signal a need to readjust expectations of each other. Here are some suggestions for healthy, non-combative conflict resolution:

TIPS AND SKILLS FOR RESOLVING CONFLICT

1. **Face the problem squarely.** The disagreement or difference of opinion will not go away just because you don't talk about it. In fact, it will only fester and grow.

2. **Actively try to understand your partner's viewpoint.** Listen intently to what he or she is saying, rather than building up ammunition for your comeback.

3. **Try the "two-question" method.** As your partner shares his or her side, ask at least one question to clarify or enhance what was said. Then, ask a second question about his or her response to your first question.

4. **Respond to the problem and/or your beloved in an honest yet caring way.** Don't allow the *tone* of your voice communicate something different than your *words.*

5. **Speak for yourself.** You are the world's greatest expert on *you.* Tell your beloved how you feel and allow him or her to do the same. It's better to get all the feelings and emotions on the table, including the negative ones, rather than trying to guess what they are.

6. **Own your feelings.** Your beloved is not the one responsible for your emotions, so you cannot expect him or her to "fix" how you are feeling.

7. **Take your share of initiative.** Don't always leave it up to your partner to raise sticky issues or propose solutions. Accept responsibility for resolving conflict.

8. **Seek "win-win" solutions.** Most conflicts can be solved through creative compromise and seeking alternative ways to meet both person's needs. If an argument ends with one winner and one loser, in the long run you both lose.

9. **Take immediate steps to implement your agreed-upon solution.** There's nothing worse than talking through a problem and then having nothing happen as a result. Even small, positive steps toward solution will make both sides feel better.

10. **Set a definite time for review.** Schedule a date and time when you can both see if the issue needs further discussion and compromise. When the time arrives be sure to check with each other that the conflict has be resolved.

People respond in different ways during a fight or disagreement. Anger and negative feelings can bring out less than positive behavior in all of us. Listed below are 10 behaviors people often use in conflict situations.

Working alone, check if each behavior characterizes you, your partner, neither of you, or both of you. Then share your answers with each other.

Finally, discuss...

A. where your perceptions about your behavior differ and why

B. how productive it is where you do agree on the nature of your behavior

C. which behaviors you might want to change.

	Me	You	Neither	Both
1. Silence				
2. Blaming				
3. Yelling				
4. Pouting				
5. Sarcasm				
6. Avoidance				
7. Appeasement				
8. Crying				
9. Threatening				
10. Physical Violence				

TRY, TRY AGAIN

Few things are more frustrating for a couple than trying to solve a simple problem together. Neither of you can fathom why the other does not recognize how wise and reasonable you are, concur with the solution you propose, and get on with other, more important, things.

This is an opportunity to take a look at how you really do come across to each other when you're in the middle of a "fight" or even a "spirited discussion." Together, choose one conflict the two of you have had recently which is still not re-solved. In a word or phrase, write the issue below. Then, working separately, try to remember your perception of how each of you handled it.

For each of the 10 questions in section A, put an "I" in the space before each response that you feel mostly closely describes your reactions and "Y" in the space before each response that you feel most closely describes your partner's reactions during your recent conflict. (You may fill in the same space for both of you on some or all of the questions.)

Name the Issue: _____

SECTION A: DURING THIS PARTICULAR CONFLICT, I FELT THAT YOU (Y) AND I (I)

1. ___denied that a problem existed   ___exaggerated the importance of the problem ___faced the problem squarely.
2. ___heard what the other was saying   ___ignored the other side.
3. ___stuck to the point   ___brought up extraneous issues.
4. ___refused to discuss   ___sought to explore the issue.
5. ___held back   ___poured forth feelings (especially negative ones).
6. ___did   ___did not accept responsibility for coping with the conflict.
7. ___tried to compromise or create alternative solutions

   ___left all the suggestions to the other person.
8. ___blamed someone else for causing the conflict   ___accepted ownership of the difficulty.
9. ___recognized what is possible   ___held to unrealistic expectations.
10. ___dealt with the conflict constructively   ___kept harping on the same points.

   Now compare your answers, discussing any surprises or differences in your perceptions. Finally, discuss each of the five steps listed in section B and see if they would help you actually resolve this particular conflict. If you think they would, then try them!

SECTION B: WHAT WOULD HAPPEN IF WE...

1. listed at least three possible options for resolving the current conflict?
2. discussed each option and then chose one together?
3. told each other how we felt about this decision?
4. tried to implement the decision?
5. agreed to discuss the matter again in two weeks?

ON OUR WORST BEHAVIOR

People respond in different ways during a fight or disagreement. Anger and negative feelings can bring out less than positive behavior in all of us. Listed below are 10 behaviors people often use in conflict situations.

Working alone, check if each behavior characterizes you, your partner, neither of you, or both of you. Then share your answers with each other.

Finally, discuss...

A. where your perceptions about your behavior differ and why

B. how productive it is where you do agree on the nature of your behavior

C. which behaviors you might want to change.

	Me	You	Neither	Both
1. Silence				
2. Blaming				
3. Yelling				
4. Pouting				
5. Sarcasm				
6. Avoidance				
7. Appeasement				
8. Crying				
9. Threatening				
10. Physical Violence				

TRY, TRY AGAIN

Few things are more frustrating for a couple than trying to solve a simple problem together. Neither of you can fathom why the other does not recognize how wise and reasonable you are, concur with the solution you propose, and get on with other, more important, things.

This is an opportunity to take a look at how you really do come across to each other when you're in the middle of a "fight" or even a "spirited discussion." Together, choose one conflict the two of you have had recently which is still not resolved. In a word or phrase, write the issue below. Then, working separately, try to remember your perception of how each of you handled it.

For each of the 10 questions in section A, put an "I" in the space before each response that you feel mostly closely describes your reactions and "Y" in the space before each response that you feel most closely describes your partner's reactions during your recent conflict. (You may fill in the same space for both of you on some or all of the questions.)

Name the Issue: _____

SECTION A: DURING THIS PARTICULAR CONFLICT, I FELT THAT YOU (Y) AND I (I)

1. ___denied that a problem existed ___exaggerated the importance of the problem ___faced the problem squarely.
2. ___heard what the other was saying ___ignored the other side.
3. ___stuck to the point ___brought up extraneous issues.
4. ___refused to discuss ___sought to explore the issue.
5. ___held back ___poured forth feelings (especially negative ones).
6. ___did ___did not accept responsibility for coping with the conflict.
7. ___tried to compromise or create alternative solutions

    ___left all the suggestions to the other person.
8. ___blamed someone else for causing the conflict ___accepted ownership of the difficulty.
9. ___recognized what is possible ___held to unrealistic expectations.
10. ___dealt with the conflict constructively ___kept harping on the same points.

   Now compare your answers, discussing any surprises or differences in your perceptions. Finally, discuss each of the five steps listed in section B and see if they would help you actually resolve this particular conflict. If you think they would, then try them!

SECTION B: WHAT WOULD HAPPEN IF WE...

1. listed at least three possible options for resolving the current conflict?
2. discussed each option and then chose one together?
3. told each other how we felt about this decision?
4. tried to implement the decision?
5. agreed to discuss the matter again in two weeks?

THE BELLS ARE RINGING

Although courtship is a happy time for most couples, the actual planning and staging of the wedding can often bring problems to an otherwise harmonious relationship. It's safe to say that a wedding can be difficult. To be successful at it, you must negotiate with each other, with your families, and with vendors, and you must implement a number of mutual decisions. The manner in which these decisions are made may provide valuable clues to the way in which you will approach other decisions later on in marriage.

Listed below are comments made by couples like yourselves who were planning their weddings. Working together, check off those things which reflect and those which do not reflect your approach to your wedding. Discuss your responses and how they reflect a decision-making style that may continue in your marriage.

OUR DECISION MAKING...

		REFLECTS	DOES NOT REFLECT
1.	"Her mother is handling everything."	_____	_____
2.	"We have divided the work evenly. She's ordering the flowers, etc.; I'll choose the band, etc."	_____	_____
3.	"He has left everything to me, because he feels that I know how everything should be."	_____	_____
4.	"My mother and I have organized most of it, with occasional suggestions from my fiancé.	_____	_____
5.	"We have both been so busy that we really haven't had a chance to get with each other to see if we have done what we agreed to do."	_____	_____
6.	"We talked about the kind of wedding we wanted, but our mothers are actually carrying out our plans."	_____	_____
7.	"She had the overall ideas for the day itself. I tried to fill in with different ways to do it or how much to spend on food, etc."	_____	_____
8.	"My fiancée and her sister literally took over what were to be our joint plans."	_____	_____
9.	"We decided how we wanted it, but needed to compromise in a few places after her parents indicated their financial limitations."	_____	_____
10.	"My fiancé travels a lot with his business, so he told me to do what I want."	_____	_____

11. "His sister just got married and his family has offered to organize things for us, too." _____ _____

12. "I think she's going overboard in many ways, but what can I say?" _____ _____

13. "I suggested a certain prayer for the ceremony, but he doesn't like it." _____ _____

14. "We were really enjoying planning our wedding until too many people started to interfere." _____ _____

15. "We set a financial limit and are juggling different options until we find a plan that works." _____ _____

16. "Our ideas about whether we want it big or small, formal or informal, morning or evening are so completely different." _____ _____

17. "According to her, I want to invite too many of my relatives." _____ _____

18. "Sometimes I wish we could just elope." _____ _____

IN DISCUSSING YOUR RESPONSES, YOU MIGHT ASK THE FOLLOWING QUESTIONS:

A. Do we work well together?

B. Are we each avoiding or accepting responsibility?

C. What is our style? Do we work well as a team?

D. Does a division of labor exist according to sex?

E. Are we taking control of our own lives and our life together?

F. How might future joint projects resemble this one? (For example, decorating and furnishing the home, planning a vacation, doing income tax, entertaining.)

As you respond to each of these questions, consider whether this is the way you want things to be throughout your marriage.

WHERE WE COME FROM

The family and home in which you grew up gave you your beginnings—physically, spiritually, psychologically, and emotionally. The impact of your family of origin is deep and pervasive, and will continue to influence you throughout your lifetime.

This influence will be quite strong in your marriage unless you consciously choose otherwise. The experience of relationship inside your family of origin will, in many ways, determine how you start a new family with your beloved. If you are like most people, the influence and "baggage" you've carried from your upbringing is a mixture of positives and negatives. These influences are expressed through values, habits, beliefs, patterns of behavior, and general outlook on life. If you don't step back and look at them, chances are these influences will continue to dictate your choices and behavior.

However, if you take time to reflect on specific ways your family has formed and shaped you in your younger years, as an adult you can more freely choose what to take with you into your new family and what you must leave behind. You can choose the values and beliefs that are truly meaningful to

you. This requires some serious reflection, and there is no better time than now to do it. Just a work of warning: Your family of origin will probably want you to take all the "baggage" with you, and so it's not uncommon to experience some tension and resistance from parents and siblings as you and your partner make deliberate choices in forming your own household and family.

This exercise is designed to help you identify the patterns of relating inside your respective families of origin. As you answer each question, check one, and only one, of the five lines under the category that best describes your view of how your family of origin operated. Your choices are **ALWAYS, USUALLY, SOMETIMES, SELDOM, NEVER.**

When finished, compare your results with your partner's. Discuss your areas of differences in experiencing growing up. Talk about how you would like your new family to function. You will likely want to come back to some of these issues to discuss them at greater length. It's important for you both to agree on how you will resolve inherited differences in relating.

	ALWAYS	USUALLY	SOMETIMES	SELDOM	NEVER
1. Did your family encourage you to express your thoughts?	—	—	—	—	—
2. Did your family encourage you to express your feelings?	—	—	—	—	—
3. Did your family members take responsibility for their actions and choices?	—	—	—	—	—
4. Were your family members encouraged to express different opinions?	—	—	—	—	—
5. Were your family members encouraged to listen to each other?	—	—	—	—	—
6. Did your family express feelings over painful issues, e.g., divorce, death, loss?	—	—	—	—	—
7. Was it acceptable in your family to express both positive and negative feelings?	—	—	—	—	—
8. Did your family support you when you tried new things?	—	—	—	—	—
9. Did your family resolve its conflicts?	—	—	—	—	—
10. Were your family members allowed to express anger constructively?	—	—	—	—	—
11. Did your family have a sense of humor?	—	—	—	—	—
12. Were your family members aware of and sensitive to each other's feelings?	—	—	—	—	—
13. Did your family encourage you to trust others outside the family?	—	—	—	—	—
14. Did your family tolerate abusive behavior (verbal, physical, sexual)?	—	—	—	—	—
15. Did your family offer each other affection, both verbally and physically?	—	—	—	—	—

This exercise is designed to surface any anxiety either of you might have about the involvement of your families of origin in your marriage. The following statements will help you clarify both your understanding of situations and your concerns about them. Equally important, they will clarify any misunderstanding you might have about your partner's reactions to both families. Remember: there is often a big difference between how you or your partner *think* (rationally, intellectually) about something and whether or not you are *bothered* (emotionally, on a feeling basis) about it, You may *think* something is true and yet not be *bothered* (apprehensive, nervous, worried, uptight) about it, or you may *feel* concerned about something even if you have no evidence that it is true.

First, mark the left side under each category—**(A) I THINK, (B) BOTHERS ME**—with your own reactions. Check one line under either "Yes," "No," or "Not Sure" for each statement under each column. Remember: the first column is what you *think* to be the case, the second column is how you truly *feel* about the situation.

When you have finished the entire list regarding your own reactions, go back and *re-read* each statement from what you believe is your partner's point of view. Then mark the right side of the list under each category—**(C) YOU THINK, (D) BOTHERS YOU**—with how you believe your partner will respond. Check one line under either "Yes," "No," or "Not Sure" for each statement under each column.

(A) I THINK			(B) BOTHERS ME				(C) YOU THINK			(D) BOTHERS YOU		
Yes	No	Not Sure	Yes	No	Not Sure		Yes	No	Not Sure	Yes	No	Not Sure
—	—	—	—	—	—	1. One or both of our families do not support our decision to marry.	—	—	—	—	—	—
—	—	—	—	—	—	2. Your family does not accept me.	—	—	—	—	—	—
—	—	—	—	—	—	3. My family does not accept you.	—	—	—	—	—	—
—	—	—	—	—	—	4. We will have difficulties in our marriage because our families are so different.	—	—	—	—	—	—
—	—	—	—	—	—	5. One or both of us has a strained relationship with parent(s) and/or family.	—	—	—	—	—	—
—	—	—	—	—	—	6. One or both of us has a particularly close relationship with mother or father.	—	—	—	—	—	—
—	—	—	—	—	—	7. One or both of our families/parents will interfere in our marital relationship.	—	—	—	—	—	—
—	—	—	—	—	—	8. One or both of our families/parents will interfere in our decisions on running our household or raising our children.	—	—	—	—	—	—
—	—	—	—	—	—	9. Our own family will be affected by having to care for one or more parents or other relatives in their old age or illness.	—	—	—	—	—	—
—	—	—	—	—	—	10. One or both of us is unwilling to discuss our role in caring for our parents or other relatives in their old age or illness.	—	—	—	—	—	—

Hold these sheets side by side and share with each other the results by comparing the answers each of you gave for A and B with those your partner gave for C and D.

If you differ on your perception of your relationships with your two families of origin (what you think is the situation), you need to discuss these items openly and honestly and decide how you are going to determine what is truly the case. If one of you has a definite concern on a specific issue or if you gave different answers regarding one another's concerns (what you feel about the situation), it means that there are anxieties which still exist regarding your families of origin with which you must still deal.

The family and home in which you grew up gave you your beginnings—physically, spiritually, psychologically, and emotionally. The impact of your family of origin is deep and pervasive, and will continue to influence you throughout your lifetime.

This influence will be quite strong in your marriage unless you consciously choose otherwise. The experience of relationship inside your family of origin will, in many ways, determine how you start a new family with your beloved. If you are like most people, the influence and "baggage" you've carried from your upbringing is a mixture of positives and negatives. These influences are expressed through values, habits, beliefs, patterns of behavior, and general outlook on life. If you don't step back and look at them, chances are these influences will continue to dictate your choices and behavior.

However, if you take time to reflect on specific ways your family has formed and shaped you in your younger years, as an adult you can more freely choose what to take with you into your new family and what you must leave behind. You can choose the values and beliefs that are truly meaningful to

you. This requires some serious reflection, and there is no better time than now to do it. Just a work of warning: Your family of origin will probably want you to take all the "baggage" with you, and so it's not uncommon to experience some tension and resistance from parents and siblings as you and your partner make deliberate choices in forming your own household and family.

This exercise is designed to help you identify the patterns of relating inside your respective families of origin. As you answer each question, check one, and only one, of the five lines under the category that best describes your view of how your family of origin operated. Your choices are **ALWAYS, USUALLY, SOMETIMES, SELDOM, NEVER.**

When finished, compare your results with your partner's. Discuss your areas of differences in experiencing growing up. Talk about how you would like your new family to function. You will likely want to come back to some of these issues to discuss them at greater length. It's important for you both to agree on how you will resolve inherited differences in relating.

	ALWAYS	USUALLY	SOMETIMES	SELDOM	NEVER
1. Did your family encourage you to express your thoughts?	—	—	—	—	—
2. Did your family encourage you to express your feelings?	—	—	—	—	—
3. Did your family members take responsibility for their actions and choices?	—	—	—	—	—
4. Were your family members encouraged to express different opinions?	—	—	—	—	—
5. Were your family members encouraged to listen to each other?	—	—	—	—	—
6. Did your family express feelings over painful issues, e.g., divorce, death, loss?	—	—	—	—	—
7. Was it acceptable in your family to express both positive and negative feelings?	—	—	—	—	—
8. Did your family support you when you tried new things?	—	—	—	—	—
9. Did your family resolve its conflicts?	—	—	—	—	—
10. Were your family members allowed to express anger constructively?	—	—	—	—	—
11. Did your family have a sense of humor?	—	—	—	—	—
12. Were your family members aware of and sensitive to each other's feelings?	—	—	—	—	—
13. Did your family encourage you to trust others outside the family?	—	—	—	—	—
14. Did your family tolerate abusive behavior (verbal, physical, sexual)?	—	—	—	—	—
15. Did your family offer each other affection, both verbally and physically?	—	—	—	—	—

MY/YOUR/OUR FAMILY

This exercise is designed to surface any anxiety either of you might have about the involvement of your families of origin in your marriage. The following statements will help you clarify both your understanding of situations and your concerns about them. Equally important, they will clarify any misunderstanding you might have about your partner's reactions to both families. Remember: there is often a big difference between how you or your partner *think* (rationally, intellectually) about something and whether or not you are *bothered* (emotionally, on a feeling basis) about it. You may *think* something is true and yet not be *bothered* (apprehensive, nervous, worried, uptight) about it, or you may *feel* concerned about something even if you have no evidence that it is true.

First, mark the left side under each category—**(A) I THINK, (B) BOTHERS ME**—with your own reactions. Check one line under either "Yes," "No," or "Not Sure" for each statement under each column. Remember: the first column is what you *think* to be the case, the second column is how you truly *feel* about the situation.

When you have finished the entire list regarding your own reactions, go back and *re-read* each statement from what you believe is your partner's point of view. Then mark the right side of the list under each category—**(C) YOU THINK, (D) BOTHERS YOU**—with how you believe your partner will respond. Check one line under either "Yes," "No," or "Not Sure" for each statement under each column.

(A) I THINK			(B) BOTHERS ME				(C) YOU THINK			(D) BOTHERS YOU		
Yes	No	Not Sure	Yes	No	Not Sure		Yes	No	Not Sure	Yes	No	Not Sure
—	—	—	—	—	—	1. One or both of our families do not support our decision to marry.	—	—	—	—	—	—
—	—	—	—	—	—	2. Your family does not accept me.	—	—	—	—	—	—
—	—	—	—	—	—	3. My family does not accept you.	—	—	—	—	—	—
—	—	—	—	—	—	4. We will have difficulties in our marriage because our families are so different.	—	—	—	—	—	—
—	—	—	—	—	—	5. One or both of us has a strained relationship with parent(s) and/or family.	—	—	—	—	—	—
—	—	—	—	—	—	6. One or both of us has a particularly close relationship with mother or father.	—	—	—	—	—	—
—	—	—	—	—	—	7. One or both of our families/parents will interfere in our marital relationship.	—	—	—	—	—	—
—	—	—	—	—	—	8. One or both of our families/parents will interfere in our decisions on running our household or raising our children.	—	—	—	—	—	—
—	—	—	—	—	—	9. Our own family will be affected by having to care for one or more parents or other relatives in their old age or illness.	—	—	—	—	—	—
—	—	—	—	—	—	10. One or both of us is unwilling to discuss our role in caring for our parents or other relatives in their old age or illness.	—	—	—	—	—	—

Hold these sheets side by side and share with each other the results by comparing the answers each of you gave for A and B with those your partner gave for C and D.

If you differ on your perception of your relationships with your two families of origin (what you think is the situation), you need to discuss these items openly and honestly and decide how you are going to determine what is truly the case. If one of you has a definite concern on a specific issue or if you gave different answers regarding one another's concerns (what you feel about the situation), it means that there are anxieties which still exist regarding your families of origin with which you must still deal.

GREAT EXPECTATIONS

Expectations—the ideas, dreams, assumptions—you have for marriage can influence your thoughts and actions in ways that can mystify your spouse. We invite you to share one expectation of either yourself, your beloved, or others in each of the following areas. Complete the list on your own, then share your responses with each other.

1. In our separate work lives, I expect...

_____

_____

_____

About this expectation, I feel:
❏ *Very Strongly*   ❏ *Let's Negotiate*   ❏ *I can take it or leave it.*

2. Regarding our leisure time together, I expect...

_____

_____

_____

About this expectation, I feel:
❏ *Very Strongly*   ❏ *Let's Negotiate*   ❏ *I can take it or leave it.*

3. Concerning our joint finances, I expect...

_____

_____

_____

About this expectation, I feel:
❏ *Very Strongly*   ❏ *Let's Negotiate*   ❏ *I can take it or leave it.*

4. With my friends, I expect...

_____

_____

_____

About this expectation, I feel:
❏ *Very Strongly*   ❏ *Let's Negotiate*   ❏ *I can take it or leave it.*

5. With your friends, I expect...

_____

_____

_____

About this expectation, I feel:
❏ *Very Strongly*   ❏ *Let's Negotiate*   ❏ *I can take it or leave it.*

6. With my family, I expect....

_____

_____

_____

About this expectation, I feel:
❏ *Very Strongly*   ❏ *Let's Negotiate*   ❏ *I can take it or leave it.*

7. With your family, I expect...

_____

_____

_____

About this expectation, I feel:

❏ *Very Strongly* ❏ *Let's Negotiate* ❏ *I can take it or leave it.*

8. As to our children, I expect...

_____

_____

_____

About this expectation, I feel:

❏ *Very Strongly* ❏ *Let's Negotiate* ❏ *I can take it or leave it.*

9. As to our individual spirituality and religious practice, I expect...

_____

_____

_____

About this expectation, I feel:

❏ *Very Strongly* ❏ *Let's Negotiate* ❏ *I can take it or leave it.*

10. As to our family traditions, I expect...

_____

_____

_____

About this expectation, I feel:

❏ *Very Strongly* ❏ *Let's Negotiate* ❏ *I can take it or leave it.*

11. Regarding our day-to-day relationship as husband and wife, I expect....

_____

_____

_____

About this expectation, I feel:

❏ *Very Strongly* ❏ *Let's Negotiate* ❏ *I can take it or leave it.*

12. Regarding our love life, I expect...

_____

_____

_____

About this expectation, I feel:

❏ *Very Strongly* ❏ *Let's Negotiate* ❏ *I can take it or leave it.*

13. Regarding my expectations, I expect...

_____

_____

_____

About this expectation, I feel:

❏ *Very Strongly* ❏ *Let's Negotiate* ❏ *I can take it or leave it.*

12. Regarding your expectations, I expect...

_____

_____

_____

About this expectation, I feel:

❏ *Very Strongly* ❏ *Let's Negotiate* ❏ *I can take it or leave it.*

GREAT EXPECTATIONS

Expectations—the ideas, dreams, assumptions—you have for marriage can influence your thoughts and actions in ways that can mystify your spouse. We invite you to share one expectation of either yourself, your beloved, or others in each of the following areas. Complete the list on your own, then share your responses with each other.

1. In our separate work lives, I expect...

_____
_____

_____

About this expectation, I feel:
❏ *Very Strongly*   ❏ *Let's Negotiate*   ❏ *I can take it or leave it.*

2. Regarding our leisure time together, I expect...

_____
_____

_____

About this expectation, I feel:
❏ *Very Strongly*   ❏ *Let's Negotiate*   ❏ *I can take it or leave it.*

3. Concerning our joint finances, I expect...

_____
_____

_____

About this expectation, I feel:
❏ *Very Strongly*   ❏ *Let's Negotiate*   ❏ *I can take it or leave it.*

4. With my friends, I expect...

_____

_____

About this expectation, I feel:
❏ *Very Strongly*   ❏ *Let's Negotiate*   ❏ *I can take it or leave it.*

5. With your friends, I expect...

_____

_____

About this expectation, I feel:
❏ *Very Strongly*   ❏ *Let's Negotiate*   ❏ *I can take it or leave it.*

6. With my family, I expect....

_____

_____

About this expectation, I feel:
❏ *Very Strongly*   ❏ *Let's Negotiate*   ❏ *I can take it or leave it.*

7. With your family, I expect...

_____

_____

_____

About this expectation, I feel:

❏ *Very Strongly*   ❏ *Let's Negotiate*   ❏ *I can take it or leave it.*

8. As to our children, I expect...

_____

_____

_____

About this expectation, I feel:

❏ *Very Strongly*   ❏ *Let's Negotiate*   ❏ *I can take it or leave it.*

9. As to our individual spirituality and religious practice, I expect...

_____

_____

_____

About this expectation, I feel:

❏ *Very Strongly*   ❏ *Let's Negotiate*   ❏ *I can take it or leave it.*

10. As to our family traditions, I expect...

_____

_____

_____

About this expectation, I feel:

❏ *Very Strongly*   ❏ *Let's Negotiate*   ❏ *I can take it or leave it.*

11. Regarding our day-to-day relationship as husband and wife, I expect....

_____

_____

_____

About this expectation, I feel:

❏ *Very Strongly*   ❏ *Let's Negotiate*   ❏ *I can take it or leave it.*

12. Regarding our love life, I expect...

_____

_____

_____

About this expectation, I feel:

❏ *Very Strongly*   ❏ *Let's Negotiate*   ❏ *I can take it or leave it.*

13. Regarding my expectations, I expect...

_____

_____

_____

About this expectation, I feel:

❏ *Very Strongly*   ❏ *Let's Negotiate*   ❏ *I can take it or leave it.*

12. Regarding your expectations, I expect...

_____

_____

_____

About this expectation, I feel:

❏ *Very Strongly*   ❏ *Let's Negotiate*   ❏ *I can take it or leave it.*

TOWARD INTIMACY

Intimacy, that special kind of total trust and friendship which marriage is all about, requires knowing the other person deeply and allowing oneself to be fully known. Achieving such mutual understanding requires attention, effort, time, and a little humility. Here is a "growth" barometer to help you judge whether you are moving toward deeper intimacy.

Depending on the stage of your relationship, fill out as many of the vertical boxes as apply (A through D). Under each of the headings (I through V) put down any number from 1 to 10. Let 1 represent a minimum amount of insight and effort and 10 represent a maximum amount. Choose and write down, as honestly as you can, the number which would best rate your development at the stated times.

Compare your responses with those of your partner and explain them to each other.

	I KNOWLEDGE OF MYSELF	II KNOWLEDGE OF MY PARTNER	III WILLINGNESS TO REVEAL MYSELF TO MY PARTNER	IV EFFORT TO KNOW MY PARTNER BETTER	V ABILITY TO BE MORE OPEN TO AND ACCEPTING OF OTHERS BECAUSE OF OUR RELATIONSHIP
A. When we first met					
B. Going together					
C. When first engaged					
D. Today					

INTIMACY CHECKUP

As a couple preparing for a marriage, you want to share all aspects of your lives to one degree or another. Below is a list of areas of intimacy in which couples can grow closer together. Rate how you think you are doing in each area and prioritize what areas you believe you need to work on. Then share the results.

In the left column, rate the importance of each area of intimacy to you:

1–not very important
2–somewhat important
3–very important
4–extremely important

In the right column, rate how strongly you feel each area of intimacy is present in your relationship right now:

1–not present
2–present to a small degree
3–present to a considerable degree
4–very strongly present

RATE 1-4   RATE 1-4

____ **A. Emotional intimacy**—feeling close, able to share our deepest thoughts, ____
hopes, and desires.

____ **B. Intellectual intimacy**—sharing our ideas, talking about current affairs, ____
literature, or any area of the human spirit.

____ **C. Sexual intimacy**—experiencing closeness and union through physical ____
sharing.

____ **D. Recreational intimacy**—having fun together in activities of mutual ____
interest, playing, and enjoying new adventures.

____ **E. Work intimacy**—sharing common tasks such as household jobs, ____
yardwork, community service projects; being interested in the other
person's daily work.

____ **F. Communication intimacy**—using good communication skills in clear, ____
honest discussions.

____ **G. Aesthetic intimacy**—appreciating the performing, written, and visual arts, ____
seeing the beauty in nature and the products of human effort.

____ **H. Crisis intimacy**—dealing together with issues ranging from the small and ____
everyday to the most difficult and troublesome.

____ **I. Commitment intimacy**—trusting each other based on faithfulness and ____
togetherness.

____ **J. Conflict intimacy**—resolving differences in a constructive manner. ____

TOWARD INTIMACY

Intimacy, that special kind of total trust and friendship which marriage is all about, requires knowing the other person deeply and allowing oneself to be fully known. Achieving such mutual understanding requires attention, effort, time, and a little humility. Here is a "growth" barometer to help you judge whether you are moving toward deeper intimacy.

Depending on the stage of your relationship, fill out as many of the vertical boxes as apply (A through D). Under each of the headings (I through V) put down any number from 1 to 10. Let 1 represent a minimum amount of insight and effort and 10 represent a maximum amount. Choose and write down, as honestly as you can, the number which would best rate your development at the stated times.

Compare your responses with those of your partner and explain them to each other.

	I KNOWLEDGE OF MYSELF	II KNOWLEDGE OF MY PARTNER	III WILLINGNESS TO REVEAL MYSELF TO MY PARTNER	IV EFFORT TO KNOW MY PARTNER BETTER	V ABILITY TO BE MORE OPEN TO AND ACCEPTING OF OTHERS BECAUSE OF OUR RELATIONSHIP
A. When we first met					
B. Going together					
C. When first engaged					
D. Today					

INTIMACY CHECKUP

As a couple preparing for a marriage, you want to share all aspects of your lives to one degree or another. Below is a list of areas of intimacy in which couples can grow closer together. Rate how you think you are doing in each area and prioritize what areas you believe you need to work on. Then share the results.

In the left column, rate the importance of each area of intimacy to you:

1–not very important
2–somewhat important
3–very important
4–extremely important

In the right column, rate how strongly you feel each area of intimacy is present in your relationship right now:

1–not present
2–present to a small degree
3–present to a considerable degree
4–very strongly present

RATE 1-4   RATE 1-4

____ **A. Emotional intimacy**—feeling close, able to share our deepest thoughts, ____
      hopes, and desires.

____ **B. Intellectual intimacy**—sharing our ideas, talking about current affairs, ____
      literature, or any area of the human spirit.

____ **C. Sexual intimacy**—experiencing closeness and union through physical ____
      sharing.

____ **D. Recreational intimacy**—having fun together in activities of mutual ____
      interest, playing, and enjoying new adventures.

____ **E. Work intimacy**—sharing common tasks such as household jobs, ____
      yardwork, community service projects; being interested in the other
      person's daily work.

____ **F. Communication intimacy**—using good communication skills in clear, ____
      honest discussions.

____ **G. Aesthetic intimacy**—appreciating the performing, written, and visual arts, ____
      seeing the beauty in nature and the products of human effort.

____ **H. Crisis intimacy**—dealing together with issues ranging from the small and ____
      everyday to the most difficult and troublesome.

____ **I. Commitment intimacy**—trusting each other based on faithfulness and ____
      togetherness.

____ **J. Conflict intimacy**—resolving differences in a constructive manner. ____

DISCOVERING EACH OTHER

A gentle exercise to help elicit important feelings that lovers might wish to discuss. Working alone, complete both column A and Column B.

After you have completed the exercise, exchange papers with your partner. Relax and compare them. Talk them over. Do any of his or her answers surprise you? Do you disagree with any of his or her answers? Are any especially interesting or thought-provoking?

	A	**B**
	Use this column to answer the following items as directly as you can.	Now, put yourself in your partner's shoes and jot down the answers you think he/she has written under column A.

1. The reason I love you

2. My strongest quality

3. My greatest weakness

4. My usual means of avoiding conflict

5. My usual means of dealing with conflict

6. My biggest worry

7. A sensitive area in which I can't take criticism

	A Your Answer	**B** What You Think Your Partner Will Answer

8. My greatest interest and concern other than our relationship

9. My definition of sexual love

10. My greatest fear about our upcoming marriage

11. The biggest adjustment I'll have to make in our first year of marriage

12. What describes us best as a couple

13. The thing I find most difficult (unpleasant, confusing) to talk about

14. Five years from now we will be

15. My feelings toward God, spirituality, and religion

DISCOVERING EACH OTHER

A gentle exercise to help elicit important feelings that lovers might wish to discuss. Working alone, complete both column A and Column B.

After you have completed the exercise, exchange papers with your partner. Relax and compare them. Talk them over. Do any of his or her answers surprise you? Do you disagree with any of his or her answers? Are any especially interesting or thought-provoking?

	A	**B**
	Use this column to answer the following items as directly as you can.	Now, put yourself in your partner's shoes and jot down the answers you think he/she has written under column A.

1. The reason I love you

2. My strongest quality

3. My greatest weakness

4. My usual means of avoiding conflict

5. My usual means of dealing with conflict

6. My biggest worry

7. A sensitive area in which I can't take criticism

	A Your Answer	**B** What You Think Your Partner Will Answer
8. My greatest interest and concern other than our relationship	_____ _____ _____	_____ _____ _____
9. My definition of sexual love	_____ _____ _____	_____ _____ _____
10. My greatest fear about our upcoming marriage	_____ _____ _____	_____ _____ _____
11. The biggest adjustment I'll have to make in our first year of marriage	_____ _____ _____	_____ _____ _____
12. What describes us best as a couple	_____ _____ _____	_____ _____ _____
13. The thing I find most difficult (unpleasant, confusing) to talk about	_____ _____ _____	_____ _____ _____
14. Five years from now we will be	_____ _____ _____	_____ _____ _____
15. My feelings toward God, spirituality, and religion	_____ _____ _____	_____ _____ _____

1 Peter and I are not very religious, and neither of us has been to church for quite a while. However, both his parents and mine are "old school" and will be crushed if we don't have a church wedding.

When we went to the rectory to make arrangements, we had a hassled discussion with the priest, who said he wouldn't marry us because we had no faith commitment. I'll admit that the idea of marriage as vocation and sacrament doesn't do anything for us, but we are baptized Catholics! The priest gave us reading materials that looked pretty dull and said he'd be willing to talk with us again.

What shall we do? Tell him what he wants to hear? Decide we'll have a civil ceremony? Or what?

- **What is the priest's point? To what does this couple object?**
- **Do you think a compromise is possible or appropriate?**

2 If my mother-in-law makes one more comment on my cooking or housekeeping, I think I will scream. She drops in two or three times a week and tells me what's wrong with my recipes; tells me why I should change furniture polish; tells me how the plant won't grow in that corner; tells me why I shouldn't spend money to have laundry done. She never speaks a word that doesn't directly or indirectly criticize me.

I keep telling Larry. He says he knows that his mother can be a pain sometimes, but he also says that I am too sensitive. Besides, he adds, I'm a big girl and can fight my own battles.

- **What do you suggest?**

3 We've been married for five months, and Susan supports trust, openness, and honesty in our marriage. I must admit that this approach is working out pretty well for us. Lately, though, she's been telling me about old boyfriends and has been asking about girls I was involved with.

I used to be sexually involved with some of the women I dated. Part of me wants to open up and tell Susan about it, if only to let her know that I love her so much more than those other women. But another part of me says: keep your mouth shut! What she doesn't know won't hurt her and can't come back to haunt me later! How much do I tell?

- **In what kinds of situations is it helpful to "tell all"?**
- **When could it be harmful?**

4 We've been married eleven weeks, and Paul has just told me he plans to spend four or five nights a month out with the boys, bowling or just drinking and talking. He says we both need our own circle of friends and that I should make similar arrangements.

I can understand occasional nights out, but this planning to be apart bothers me. I married Paul to be with him and to do things together. Besides, my girl friends don't go out much without their husbands.

- **Why might she be reacting to the "planning?"**
- **What's better for a couple—separate friends or only mutual ones?**

5 When I came home from shopping last Saturday, Bill informed me that his sister had just called and that he had agreed to go over for drinks and hamburgers in her backyard. I like his sister very much, but I feel my husband has no right making social commitments without checking with me first. He could just as easily have said, "I'll see if Julie has anything planned and call you back." This is about the third time Bill has done something like this during the nine months we've been married.

When we talked about it later, he said, "We had no plans, and you should not be disturbed in an informal situation like this. If you really didn't want to go, it would have been easy to call and cancel."

- **Is Bill off base, or is Julie too rigid?**
- **What might prevent these kinds of problems for a couple?**

6 Julie's faith is very important to her. She goes to church every Sunday and attends a faith-sharing group one evening a week. Chad, on the other, doesn't have the least interest in religion. In fact, because of less than positive experiences as a child and teenager, his attitude toward church is downright negative. Julie and Chad avoid talking about this difference between them because it always causes conflict. But Julie continues to pray for Chad, and she is hopeful that once they are married and start a family he will change his attitude and see the importance of religion.

- **Should Chad be more open to and tolerant of religion?**
- **Are Julie's hopes and expectations realistic?**

7 Our wedding is only a couple of months away, and I have a problem. Any time something irritates or displeases Ellen, she withdraws. By now, I can tell her mood immediately, but it's always an uphill battle: first, to get her to admit there is a problem, then to find out what it is, and finally, to discuss it reasonably.

I come from a big family, and I can handle noise and fights, but silence frustrates and angers me. She says she just doesn't like to argue, and if I would just ignore her moods, we would get along better. She says I push too much to find out what she is thinking. I say I ignoring her in these moods would be like ignoring a booby trap.

- **What can a partner's silence communicate?**
- **How could he approach Ellen in a better way?**

8 I love Judy very much. But in recent months she has changed, and I'm not sure how to deal with it. Shortly after she started her new job she became much more outspoken and assertive with her ideas and opinions, especially with the way our society treats women. Sometimes I feel like she blames me personally for all of society's ills, just because I'm a man. I don't consider myself sexist, and I don't want Judy to be passive and submissive, but her aggressive attitudes and strong opinions are affecting our relationship.

- **Whose problem is this: his, hers or theirs?**
- **What would you suggest he say to Judy?**

9 Before we were married we both agreed to delay having children in order to save money. Tonight, on the way home from my nephew's baptism, Michele mentioned how nice it might be to have a baby. It's not that I don't like kids. As a matter of fact, while I was holding my nephew, I got a warm feeling. And, Michele would make a fantastic mother. But something says, "Tom, are you really ready to take on that kind of responsibility?" I don't know the answer.

- **What are responsible reasons for having children?**
- **How does a couple know when they're ready?**

10 During our courtship and engagement, I really liked Art's easy-going manner. No matter what, he remained cool, calm, and collected. However, now that we've been married a while, this easy-going attitude is starting to irritate me. At times, I wish he would blow up so I would know what's bothering him. I even feel that he's letting me make all the decisions. Some time I'd love to hear him say, "Linda, this is what we're going to do!" Should I think my lucky stars that I married a guy like Art? Or could something be seriously wrong?

- **How do you think Linda views Art's feelings toward her?**
- **Why is a quality she liked in Art before marriage something that irritates her now?**

11 Tom and Ann have been married almost a year. Both have professional jobs with lots of responsibility. They enjoy their careers and each has worked hard to advance within their respective companies. Yesterday, Ann came home full of excitement. She's been offered a terrific promotion, a two-step jump on the company pay scale, increased responsibilities as a supervisor, and a much larger office with a window. "Wow, Ann that's fantastic!" Tom says. He claims he is genuinely pleased for her...at least until Ann tells him it all means they would have to move across the country to the home office. Tom's company doesn't have an office in that city. He'd have to start over with another company.

- **How do you suggest Tom and Ann work out this dilemma?**
- **What if Tom got the promotion and Ann had to start over?**

12 Although my husband and I communicate with one another fairly well, sex is one area about which we can't seem to talk. Lately, it has become a source of real tension. I know Bill wants to please me, but he always seems to assume he knows what pleases me. He takes any sign of affection on my part to be an invitation to intercourse. If I indicate no, he pouts and sulks. Sometimes I have the feeling that he has an unrealistic ideal about how he should be as a lover. I can't go on like this much longer.

- **Why is it so hard to talk about sex sometimes?**

SHARING THE FAITH VISION

Religious faith brings strength to each partner in a marriage. Sharing your spiritual beliefs can strengthen your marital love and relationship. Reflecting upon and discussing your religious attitudes, concerns, and questions prior to marriage will surely enhance your respect for and understanding of each other.

Use the reflections questions below to guide your discussion. Take time separately to write your responses, and then share your feelings as openly and freely as you can. If any of your responses or discussions raise concerns, you might want to discuss them with your priest, minister, rabbi, or imam.

1. On a scale of 1-10 (10 being most spiritual), I would rate myself this spiritual _____

2. One positive spiritual/religious experience I've had is _____
_____
_____

3. One negative experience that turned me off is_____
_____
_____

4. When I pray, I _____
_____
_____
_____

5. In terms of my marriage, I would like to ask God for _____
_____
_____

6. My faith helps me in my life and in my relationship with my beloved by _____
_____
_____
_____

7. I hope to share my faith and beliefs with my future spouse by _____
_____
_____
_____

8. My reasons for marrying in a religious ceremony are _____
_____
_____
_____

9. I contribute to the life of my church, synagogue, or mosque _____
_____
_____
_____

10. Some of my questions, doubts and confusions about religion and faith are _____
_____
_____
_____
_____

11. On a scale of 1-10 (10 being most satisfied), how satisfied are you with your response to question #1?_____

FOR INTERFAITH COUPLES

Marriages in which a Catholic marries a non-Catholic are commonplace today. Studies reveal some important findings about interfaith marriages:

Attitudes toward interfaith marriages are becoming much more favorable.

Religious differences within a marriage do tend to reduce marital satisfaction and decrease church involvement.

Disagreement over children's religious upbringing is one of the most common causes of strife in interfaith marriages.

Interfaith marriages have a higher percentage of divorce than same-faith marriages.

While some of these statistics may be unsettling, an interfaith couple who possess a loving, nonjudgmental relationship can live a truly fruitful marriage while functioning as a symbol of acceptance and cooperation for others. If you are an interfaith couple, be sure to reflect on and discuss the questions below and read *Two Faiths, One Love* on page 39.

1. Sharing my faith and religious beliefs with my partner will benefit our marriage by _____

_____

_____

_____

2. Some potential religious issues or questions that might create problems for us are _____

_____

_____

_____

3. We should handle the question of religious upbringing of our children by _____

_____

_____

_____

_____

_____

_____

_____

SHARING THE FAITH VISION

Religious faith brings strength to each partner in a marriage. Sharing your spiritual beliefs can strengthen your marital love and relationship. Reflecting upon and discussing your religious attitudes, concerns, and questions prior to marriage will surely enhance your respect for and understanding of each other.

Use the reflections questions below to guide your discussion. Take time separately to write your responses, and then share your feelings as openly and freely as you can. If any of your responses or discussions raise concerns, you might want to discuss them with your priest, minister, rabbi, or imam.

1. On a scale of 1-10 (10 being most spiritual), I would rate myself this spiritual _____

2. One positive spiritual/religious experience I've had is _____

_____

_____

3. One negative experience that turned me off is _____

_____

_____

4. When I pray, I _____

_____

_____

_____

5. In terms of my marriage, I would like to ask God for _____

_____

_____

_____

6. My faith helps me in my life and in my relationship with my beloved by _____

_____

_____

_____

7. I hope to share my faith and beliefs with my future spouse by _____

_____

_____

_____

8. My reasons for marrying in a religious ceremony are _____

_____

_____

_____

9. I contribute to the life of my church, synagogue, or mosque _____

_____

_____

_____

10. Some of my questions, doubts and confusions about religion and faith are _____

_____

_____

_____

_____

_____

11. On a scale of 1-10 (10 being most satisfied), how satisfied are you with your response to question #1? _____

FOR INTERFAITH COUPLES

Marriages in which a Catholic marries a non-Catholic are commonplace today. Studies reveal some important findings about interfaith marriages:

Attitudes toward interfaith marriages are becoming much more favorable.

Religious differences within a marriage do tend to reduce marital satisfaction and decrease church involvement.

Disagreement over children's religious upbringing is one of the most common causes of strife in interfaith marriages.

Interfaith marriages have a higher percentage of divorce than same-faith marriages.

While some of these statistics may be unsettling, an interfaith couple who possess a loving, nonjudgmental relationship can live a truly fruitful marriage while functioning as a symbol of acceptance and cooperation for others. If you are an interfaith couple, be sure to reflect on and discuss the questions below and read *Two Faiths, One Love* on page 39.

1. Sharing my faith and religious beliefs with my partner will benefit our marriage by _____

_____

_____

_____

2. Some potential religious issues or questions that might create problems for us are _____

_____

_____

_____

3. We should handle the question of religious upbringing of our children by _____

_____

_____

_____

_____

_____

_____

_____

Many marriages today involve two peoples from different religious backgrounds. This might include two Christians from different denominations, two people from totally different faiths, or even two peoples of the same religious tradition where one person's faith is very fervent and one's is not. Such couples usually realize—and official teaching of most religions have long insisted—that such "interfaith" marriages can be fraught with special dangers.

Those interfaith couples who do not deal with their religious differences can find themselves studiously avoiding all religious questions and drifting into spiritual indifference, thereby losing an essential part of their individual lives and a major source of a richer life together. They also are a source of confusion for their children, who grow up not knowing "what to believe."

If you two do not share the same religious beliefs and practices, you will have to work and pray hard to realize the potential special blessings of your marriage. Rather than ignoring your differences, celebrate them. Here are some practical suggestions.

1 Encourage your partner in his or her religious pursuits and practices. Help each other keep in touch with the sources of grace and inspiration that each finds most useful. Because these practices will help each partner become his or her best self, they can only enrich and benefit your relationship.

2 Attend the other's worship services occasionally. Try to understand the experience and tradition from which your partner's faith life has come. As a joint statement of Catholic, Protestant, and Jewish leaders puts it, "This attendance is in no sense a compromise. Love requires knowledge of the beloved."

3 Try to get to know and understand some of your partner's fellow congregation members.

4 If there are social groups or study clubs affiliated with your individual congregations that hold some interest for you, become involved together. Sometimes you might wish to jointly attend special events like conferences, retreats, or ecumenical celebrations.

5 Give some practical consideration to your religious observance during the first few weeks of marriage. How will you schedule your time, responsibility, transportation, etc. so you can attend services? After a while, convenient patterns will develop, but some forethought might be required in the beginning.

6 Although you cannot blend your two different belief systems completely, you can certainly build a common spirituality that is meaningful to you both.

7 Learn to pray together with some regularity. Pray about your lives, your hopes, and your needs; pray for the people dear to you, for those in great need, and about some of the critical questions facing all of us today. Determine some of the occasions, set some times of the day or week, when you can pray together.

8 Perhaps you can use some prayers from each partner's faith tradition, some that you hold in common, and even new ones that you create to express special meanings for you and your marriage. In addition, there are many new, well-designed books of prayer and meditation that both of you will find very nourishing.

9 Consider the religious rituals and customs that could be woven into your family life. Perhaps those that surround holy days from each of your traditions or non-religious holidays such as Thanksgiving and Memorial Day might be a good place to start. Make a list of customs that have meaning for each of you. Discuss the various ways your families handled holidays and celebrations and see which ones might be suitable for your new family. Rituals give depth and richness to our lives because they remind us of meanings beyond daily routine. They don't just happen, however; you must work at them.

10 Become involved as a couple in some charitable or service-oriented projects assisting the poor, the aged, children, etc. This could be a manifestation of your shared, but different, faiths.

11 Confront the problem of the religious upbringing of your children honestly and early in your marriage. Realize that no perfect solution exists, but bear in mind that children require a consistent faith that tells them the meaning of the world. They need symbols, prayers, and practices that allow that faith to take root and have expression.

PLEASE LISTEN TO ME

Here is a letter written by an unknown author to his or her future spouse. Perhaps you would like to give a copy to yours. Or, better yet, write one of your own.

My Beloved,

When I ask you to listen to me and you start giving advice, you have not done what I asked. When I ask you to listen to me and you begin to tell me why I shouldn't feel that way, you are telling me to deny my feelings. When I ask you to listen to me and you feel you have to do something to solve my problems, you have failed me (strange as that may seem).

Listen. All I ask is that you listen. Not talk or do, just hear me. The giving of advice can never take the place of the giving of yourself. I'm not helpless...or hopeless!

When you do something for me that I need to do for myself, you contribute to my fear...and weakness. But when you accept the simple fact that I do feel what I feel (no matter how irrational that may seem), then I quit trying to convince you and can get on with trying to understand what's behind my feelings. And when I do, the answers become obvious. And you know what? Your listening made that possible.

Feelings make sense when we try to understand what's behind them. That's why prayer works—sometimes—for people, because God is still and doesn't give advice or try to fix things. God just listens and lets you work it out for yourself, staying your "silent partner."

So please listen and just hear me. There are important times in our lives when we just need to be heard...not cured.

In anticipation,

Your future spouse.

One of the most important tasks facing your relationship is the creation of a new family. Greater scientific awareness has made it possible to prevent or encourage conception of babies safely and naturally. Medical progress has also meant that babies with disabilities now survive more readily. You might be called to raise a disabled child yourselves. There is also a need for more adoptive and foster homes for children with special needs. That too may be part of the gift of your marriage. It is your responsibility as a married couple to decide the nature of your own family in light of the teachings of your church or your moral beliefs.

It is not too early to make some of these decisions, even though as you change and grow as a couple and a family you should continually reevaluate them with an attitude of love and openness to life.

Problems in marriage arise as often from misunderstandings as from differences of opinion. This is never more true than over issues involving children. The following is a quick and easy exercise to confirm that you both have the same understandings about having and raising children, even though these understandings will certainly grow and mature over the years. On issues like these, don't assume that you have reached accord unless you have specifically done so.

For each issue, answer these two questions: **Have you discussed this matter to your satisfaction? Have you agree upon an answer for the time being?**

Check one line under either **Yes**, **No**, or **Not Sure** for each issue under each column.

HAVE WE DISCUSSED?   /   HAVE WE AGREED UPON?

Yes No Not Sure

1. Having children?
2. Whether we are prepared to be parents?
3. The number of children we want?
4. How—if at all—we will attempt to space our children's births?
5. When we would like to begin having children?
6. Not being able to have children of our own?
7. The possibility of adopting or fostering children?
8. The possibility of raising a disabled child?
9. Our beliefs about the way to discipline children?
10. The future education of our children?
11. The religious upbringing of our children?

Compare your responses. Where there is disagreement or where either of you has answered "Not Sure," there is need for further discussion both before and after the wedding. These questions are too important to ignore. You might want to save this exercise and redo it each year on your anniversary, just to make sure you're both on the same wavelength regarding the development of your family.

ARE WE READY?

This exercise is designed to help you see how prepared you are to become parents. Working separately, complete each statement about your future family. Write phrases or sentences rather than one word responses, so your beloved can get a full and clear sense of your feelings about parenting.

When finished, share the results with your partner. Focus on those issues about which you have important concerns or differences and discuss how you will resolve them.

---

1. When I think about the way I was parented as a child, I hope I can _____

_____

_____

_____

_____

2. Three positive qualities I think I will have as a parent _____

_____

_____

_____

_____

3. My greatest concern about being a good parent _____

_____

_____

_____

_____

4. Three positive qualities I think you will have as a parent _____

_____

_____

_____

5. My greatest concern about your ability to be a good parent _____

_____

_____

_____

_____

6. The primary attitudes and behaviors I want to cultivate in our children _____

_____

_____

_____

_____

7. We can prepare ourselves for parenthood by _____

_____

_____

_____

_____

8. Role models and resources we can turn to for help _____

_____

_____

_____

One of the most important tasks facing your relationship is the creation of a new family. Greater scientific awareness has made it possible to prevent or encourage conception of babies safely and naturally. Medical progress has also meant that babies with disabilities now survive more readily. You might be called to raise a disabled child yourselves. There is also a need for more adoptive and foster homes for children with special needs. That too may be part of the gift of your marriage. It is your responsibility as a married couple to decide the nature of your own family in light of the teachings of your church or your moral beliefs.

It is not too early to make some of these decisions, even though as you change and grow as a couple and a family you should continually reevaluate them with an attitude of love and openness to life.

Problems in marriage arise as often from misunderstandings as from differences of opinion. This is never more true than over issues involving children. The following is a quick and easy exercise to confirm that you both have the same understandings about having and raising children, even though these understandings will certainly grow and mature over the years. On issues like these, don't assume that you have reached accord unless you have specifically done so.

For each issue, answer these two questions: **Have you discussed this matter to your satisfaction? Have you agree upon an answer for the time being?**

Check one line under either **Yes**, **No**, or **Not Sure** for each issue under each column.

HAVE WE DISCUSSED?					HAVE WE AGREED UPON?		
Yes	No	Not Sure			Yes	No	Not Sure
—	—	—	1. Having children?		—	—	—
—	—	—	2. Whether we are prepared to be parents?		—	—	—
—	—	—	3. The number of children we want?		—	—	—
—	—	—	4. How—if at all—we will attempt to space our children's births?		—	—	—
—	—	—	5. When we would like to begin having children?		—	—	—
—	—	—	6. Not being able to have children of our own?		—	—	—
—	—	—	7. The possibility of adopting or fostering children?		—	—	—
—	—	—	8. The possibility of raising a disabled child?		—	—	—
—	—	—	9. Our beliefs about the way to discipline children?		—	—	—
—	—	—	10. The future education of our children?		—	—	—
—	—	—	11. The religious upbringing of our children?		—	—	—

Compare your responses. Where there is disagreement or where either of you has answered "Not Sure," there is need for further discussion both before and after the wedding. These questions are too important to ignore. You might want to save this exercise and redo it each year on your anniversary, just to make sure you're both on the same wavelength regarding the development of your family.

ARE WE READY?

This exercise is designed to help you see how prepared you are to become parents. Working separately, complete each statement about your future family. Write phrases or sentences rather than one word responses, so your beloved can get a full and clear sense of your feelings about parenting.

When finished, share the results with your partner. Focus on those issues about which you have important concerns or differences and discuss how you will resolve them.

---

1. When I think about the way I was parented as a child, I hope I can _____

_____

_____

_____

_____

2. Three positive qualities I think I will have as a parent _____

_____

_____

_____

_____

3. My greatest concern about being a good parent _____

_____

_____

_____

_____

4. Three positive qualities I think you will have as a parent _____

_____

_____

_____

_____

5. My greatest concern about your ability to be a good parent_____

_____

_____

_____

_____

6. The primary attitudes and behaviors I want to cultivate in our children _____

_____

_____

_____

_____

7. We can prepare ourselves for parenthood by _____

_____

_____

_____

_____

8. Role models and resources we can turn to for help _____

_____

_____

_____

_____

TAKE THIS JOB

There are many tasks that need to be done around the house in a marriage. Some of them are paid, most of them are not. Most of us have been raised to expect that certain jobs are done primarily by males and others done mostly by females. It will be helpful to be clear before you get married who is going to do what. But keep in mind that deciding who will do these jobs now doesn't mean you cannot change assignments later in your marriage. Many couples shift their roles and responsibilities several times throughout the years of their marriage.

Listed below are some common household chores (there is room to add others before you get started). Working separately, mark under the correct column who you think should **(S)** and who you think will **(W)**—it's not always the same!—perform each task in your marriage. Then share the results with your partner. Discuss those areas where you have different ideas.

JOB	EITHER	BOTH	MALE	FEMALE	NEITHER	HIRE SOMEONE ELSE
1. Taking out the garbage						
2. Doing the dishes						
3. Making the bed						
4. Mowing the lawn						
5. Cooking dinner						
6. Vacuuming, dusting						
7. Scrubbing floors						
8. Washing windows						
9. Painting the house						
10. Making breakfast						
11. Grocery shopping						
12. Fixing the car						
13. Taking out the dog (cat)						
14. Ironing						
15. Preparing lunch						
16. Straightening the basement						
17. Keeping the checkbook						
18. Decorating the home						
19. Doing the laundry						
20. Cleaning the bathroom						
21. Gardening						
22. Shoveling snow						
23. Minor home repairs						
24.						
25.						

BEAT THE CLOCK

Like money, time is a measure of what we value. There are only 24 hours in a day, 168 hours in a week. Do you and your partner understand and agree on how you will each use this highly prized asset when you are married?

Working alone, look over each of the following activities. Before you begin, add any other major time-consuming activities on the lines provided at the end of the list. Then estimate in the column on the right the number of hours on the average you anticipate you yourself will spend during the first year of marriage on each activities during a regular, non-vacation, non-crisis week. (If you feel you can do two things at once, put the time under one category only.)

Add your hours together and put the total at the bottom. Adjust your estimates until your total is exactly 168! Finally, share your list with your partner and discuss any surprises you find on each other's list.

ACTIVITY	HOURS PER WEEK
1. Sleeping	
2. Preparing and eating meals at home	
3. Exercising, sports, and personal care	
4. Paid jobs, including commuting	
5. Housework tasks and chores	
6. Shopping and other errands	
7. Childcare	
8. Studying and reading	
9. Watching TV and movies at home	
10. Praying and worshiping	
11. Volunteer activities	
12. Visiting family and friends	
13. Going out for entertainment or meals (together)	
14. Going out for entertainment or meals (without your partner)	
15. Hobbies (together)	
16. Hobbies (without your partner)	
17. Talking, cuddling, making love	
18. Doing nothing	
19.	
20.	
	TOTAL

TAKE THIS JOB

There are many tasks that need to be done around the house in a marriage. Some of them are paid, most of them are not. Most of us have been raised to expect that certain jobs are done primarily by males and others done mostly by females. It will be helpful to be clear before you get married who is going to do what. But keep in mind that deciding who will do these jobs now doesn't mean you cannot change assignments later in your marriage. Many couples shift their roles and responsibilities several times throughout the years of their marriage.

Listed below are some common household chores (there is room to add others before you get started). Working separately, mark under the correct column who you think should **(S)** and who you think will **(W)**—it's not always the same!—perform each task in your marriage. Then share the results with your partner. Discuss those areas where you have different ideas.

JOB	EITHER	BOTH	MALE	FEMALE	NEITHER	HIRE SOMEONE ELSE
1. Taking out the garbage						
2. Doing the dishes						
3. Making the bed						
4. Mowing the lawn						
5. Cooking dinner						
6. Vacuuming, dusting						
7. Scrubbing floors						
8. Washing windows						
9. Painting the house						
10. Making breakfast						
11. Grocery shopping						
12. Fixing the car						
13. Taking out the dog (cat)						
14. Ironing						
15. Preparing lunch						
16. Straightening the basement						
17. Keeping the checkbook						
18. Decorating the home						
19. Doing the laundry						
20. Cleaning the bathroom						
21. Gardening						
22. Shoveling snow						
23. Minor home repairs						
24.						
25.						

BEAT THE CLOCK

Like money, time is a measure of what we value. There are only 24 hours in a day, 168 hours in a week. Do you and your partner understand and agree on how you will each use this highly prized asset when you are married?

Working alone, look over each of the following activities. Before you begin, add any other major time-consuming activities on the lines provided at the end of the list. Then estimate in the column on the right the number of hours on the average you anticipate you yourself will spend during the first year of marriage on each activities during a regular, non-vacation, non-crisis week. (If you feel you can do two things at once, put the time under one category only.)

Add your hours together and put the total at the bottom. Adjust your estimates until your total is exactly 168! Finally, share your list with your partner and discuss any surprises you find on each other's list.

ACTIVITY	HOURS PER WEEK
1. Sleeping	
2. Preparing and eating meals at home	
3. Exercising, sports, and personal care	
4. Paid jobs, including commuting	
5. Housework tasks and chores	
6. Shopping and other errands	
7. Childcare	
8. Studying and reading	
9. Watching TV and movies at home	
10. Praying and worshiping	
11. Volunteer activities	
12. Visiting family and friends	
13. Going out for entertainment or meals (together)	
14. Going out for entertainment or meals (without your partner)	
15. Hobbies (together)	
16. Hobbies (without your partner)	
17. Talking, cuddling, making love	
18. Doing nothing	
19.	
20.	
TOTAL	

ALCOHOL & DRUGS

Alcohol and drug abuse are leading causes of problems in marriage...often leading to separation and divorce. The abuse of alcohol or drugs (both illegal and prescription) is a deep-seated problem that will not go away by itself. Such behavior before marriage will only worsen with the added responsibility of marriage and family. If you are even slightly concerned about your own or your partner's use of alcohol or drugs, *deal with it now.*

Working alone, place a check mark in the appropriate column after the following 20 questions if the statement is even slightly true for yourself or—to the best of your knowledge—for your future spouse. If you are unsure of your response to any question put a question mark in the appropriate column. When you are finished, share your responses with each other. If either of you (or both) have several check or question marks, you should definitely discuss your concerns with each other, seek more information, and get some help before the wedding.

	TRUE FOR ME	TRUE FOR MY PARTNER
1. Do either of you lose time from work because of drinking or using drugs?	_____	_____
2. Is drinking or drug use making either of your lives unhappy in any way?	_____	_____
3. Do either of you drink or use drugs because you are shy or uncomfortable around other people?	_____	_____
4. Is drinking or drug use affecting either of your reputations?	_____	_____
5. Have either of you gotten into financial difficulties as a result of drinking or using drugs?	_____	_____
6. Do either of you turn to different companions or an inferior environment when drinking or using drugs?	_____	_____
7. Do either of you need to get "high" at a definite time each day or week?	_____	_____
8. Do either of you want a "chaser" the next morning after partying?	_____	_____
9. Has alcohol or drugs ever caused either of you to have difficulty sleeping?	_____	_____
10. Do either of you drink or take drugs to escape from worries or trouble?	_____	_____
11. Do either of you drink or take drugs to build up your self-confidence?	_____	_____
12. Have either of you ever been concerned about your own or your partner's drinking or use of drugs?	_____	_____
13. Have either of you ever extracted promises about drinking or drug use from the other that were not kept?	_____	_____
14. Have either of you made threats or decisions because of the other's use of alcohol or drugs?	_____	_____

15. Do either of you feel responsible for or guilty about the other's use of alcohol or drugs?   _____   _____

16. Do either of you try to conceal your own or the other's drinking or use of drugs, or deny there is a problem despite strong evidence of its existence?   _____   _____

17. Have either of you ever avoided activities with families and friends because of fear of embarrassment over the other's use of alcohol or drugs?   _____   _____

18. Have either of you ever felt the need to justify to someone else your own, or your partner's, use of alcohol or drugs?   _____   _____

19. Do either of you exhibit any physical symptoms such as nausea, a "knot" in the stomach, ulcers, shakiness, sweating palms, or bitten fingernails because of your own or your partner's drinking or use of drugs?   _____   _____

20. Do either of you feel helpless about your own or your partner's use of alcohol or drugs—that nothing you or anyone else can do will make the situation better?   _____   _____

If you are even slightly concerned about your own or your partner's use of alcohol or drugs, *talk to someone now.* You're only fooling yourself if you think the problem will resolve itself after you're married. Whom can you talk to? Start with a friend, parent, sibling, or co-worker and ask for an opinion and advice. You can also speak to a member of the clergy for support and referral information. Or call a local social service agency whose trained counselors will offer expert assistance. We cannot say it more bluntly. *This is a serious issue that the two of you will not be able to solve by yourselves!* Seek the help you need *now.*

A NOTE ON PHYSICAL ABUSE WITHIN MARRIAGE

One of the by-products of alcohol and drug abuse is often physical abuse. Physical abuse is something we sometimes joke about ("To the moon, Alice..."), but it is more serious and widespread than many realize. Physical abuse happens among all classes and ethnic groups, regardless of their income and educational levels. Violence in the home usually becomes more frequent and serious over time. It is part of an escalating pattern that begins with threats, insults, explosive tempers, and attempts to isolate or overpower the other.

Children from violent homes learn to regard violence as an acceptable means of control and a normal way of responding to disappointment and frustration. When they grow up, these children are very likely to become either victims of abuse or abusers themselves.

Like alcohol and drug abuse, physical abuse needs to be dealt with if it is part of your relationship. If you need help, get it now—before the wedding. The one thing that is sure is that the problem will not go away after you are married.

ALCOHOL & DRUGS

Alcohol and drug abuse are leading causes of problems in marriage...often leading to separation and divorce. The abuse of alcohol or drugs (both illegal and prescription) is a deep-seated problem that will not go away by itself. Such behavior before marriage will only worsen with the added responsibility of marriage and family. If you are even slightly concerned about your own or your partner's use of alcohol or drugs, *deal with it now*.

Working alone, place a check mark in the appropriate column after the following 20 questions if the statement is even slightly true for yourself or—to the best of your knowledge—for your future spouse. If you are unsure of your response to any question put a question mark in the appropriate column. When you are finished, share your responses with each other. If either of you (or both) have several check or question marks, you should definitely discuss your concerns with each other, seek more information, and get some help before the wedding.

	TRUE FOR ME	TRUE FOR MY PARTNER
1. Do either of you lose time from work because of drinking or using drugs?	_____	_____
2. Is drinking or drug use making either of your lives unhappy in any way?	_____	_____
3. Do either of you drink or use drugs because you are shy or uncomfortable around other people?	_____	_____
4. Is drinking or drug use affecting either of your reputations?	_____	_____
5. Have either of you gotten into financial difficulties as a result of drinking or using drugs?	_____	_____
6. Do either of you turn to different companions or an inferior environment when drinking or using drugs?	_____	_____
7. Do either of you need to get "high" at a definite time each day or week?	_____	_____
8. Do either of you want a "chaser" the next morning after partying?	_____	_____
9. Has alcohol or drugs ever caused either of you to have difficulty sleeping?	_____	_____
10. Do either of you drink or take drugs to escape from worries or trouble?	_____	_____
11. Do either of you drink or take drugs to build up your self-confidence?	_____	_____
12. Have either of you ever been concerned about your own or your partner's drinking or use of drugs?	_____	_____
13. Have either of you ever extracted promises about drinking or drug use from the other that were not kept?	_____	_____
14. Have either of you made threats or decisions because of the other's use of alcohol or drugs?	_____	_____

15. Do either of you feel responsible for or guilty about the other's use of alcohol or drugs? _____ _____

16. Do either of you try to conceal your own or the other's drinking or use of drugs, or deny there is a problem despite strong evidence of its existence? _____ _____

17. Have either of you ever avoided activities with families and friends because of fear of embarrassment over the other's use of alcohol or drugs? _____ _____

18. Have either of you ever felt the need to justify to someone else your own, or your partner's, use of alcohol or drugs? _____ _____

19. Do either of you exhibit any physical symptoms such as nausea, a "knot" in the stomach, ulcers, shakiness, sweating palms, or bitten fingernails because of your own or your partner's drinking or use of drugs? _____ _____

20. Do either of you feel helpless about your own or your partner's use of alcohol or drugs—that nothing you or anyone else can do will make the situation better? _____ _____

If you are even slightly concerned about your own or your partner's use of alcohol or drugs, *talk to someone now.* You're only fooling yourself if you think the problem will resolve itself after you're married. Whom can you talk to? Start with a friend, parent, sibling, or co-worker and ask for an opinion and advice. You can also speak to a member of the clergy for support and referral information. Or call a local social service agency whose trained counselors will offer expert assistance. We cannot say it more bluntly. *This is a serious issue that the two of you will not be able to solve by yourselves!* Seek the help you need *now.*

A NOTE ON PHYSICAL ABUSE WITHIN MARRIAGE

One of the by-products of alcohol and drug abuse is often physical abuse. Physical abuse is something we sometimes joke about ("To the moon, Alice..."), but it is more serious and widespread than many realize. Physical abuse happens among all classes and ethnic groups, regardless of their income and educational levels. Violence in the home usually becomes more frequent and serious over time. It is part of an escalating pattern that begins with threats, insults, explosive tempers, and attempts to isolate or overpower the other.

Children from violent homes learn to regard violence as an acceptable means of control and a normal way of responding to disappointment and frustration. When they grow up, these children are very likely to become either victims of abuse or abusers themselves.

Like alcohol and drug abuse, physical abuse needs to be dealt with if it is part of your relationship. If you need help, get it now—before the wedding. The one thing that is sure is that the problem will not go away after you are married.

THE DOLLAR ALMIGHTY?

Like the flag, a kiss, the cross, or a four-letter word, money is a powerful symbol. Having it can mean security, status, comfort, freedom, control, acceptance. The lack of it can mean fear, depression, inferiority, guilt, anxiety. Discuss the following questions together.

What are your individual attitudes on money?

How has your experience in your own families of origin formed your individual attitudes?

How will money matters be handled in your marriage? (Who will keep the checkbook? Pay the bills? Do the banking? Make investment decisions?)

How are you going to communicate about money: When crises arise? At set intervals (daily, weekly, monthly, yearly)?

Will you share your money with others? How? How much? When? With whom?

TWO INCOMES

Most couples getting married today have two careers and incomes. You need to discuss if this will always be the case in your marriage. Might you decide to go to a single income when children arrive or in order for one of you to attend school or for some other reason? If so, then you need to plan for that change now. Will you enjoy the benefits of two incomes on a short-term basis or will you save the "extra" money you earn now for later?

THREE COUPLES TO PITY

Couple #1: Believe time is money. They know the price of everything but the value of nothing. They would sell their souls for the right price. They are dead in spirit years before they have the good grace to lie down.

Couple #2: Believe the world owes them a living. They despise work and have no realization that humans are called to contribute to the ongoing creation of the universe. They are parasites—sometimes attractive, intelligent or highly entertaining—but parasites nonetheless.

Couple #3: Have good intentions but are undisciplined and unreflective. They fall prey to every desire excited in them by advertisers and the media. They overstretch their credit, overestimate their earnings, underestimate their bills, and never dream of planning or budgeting.

POSSESS OR BE POSSESSED

You are possessed by the things you possess. They claim your time and effort in paying for them; they sap your emotional and physical energy in worrying about them, protecting them, caring for them; they fill your imagination with dreams of how to get more of them.

The first fruit of poverty of spirit, of detachment, of schooling yourself in not wanting more things, is freedom.

If you are truly in love, your love for each other will want to burst out of your relationship—like new wine in old wineskins. You will start to give, not take. The best gift you can give is yourselves—your time, your interest, your talents—to projects, to works of compassion, to worthy causes. Nor can you ignore your treasure (however meager it may be at the moment)! If you are truly thankful for the blessing of your love, you will want to share your possessions with those less fortunate than you.

Give as if your marriage depended on it. It does.

YOUR FINANCIAL HOUSE

"A loaf of bread, a jug of wine, and thou beside me singing in the wilderness, and wilderness were paradise enough!" This famous line from *The Rubaiyat* is used at many weddings. It sums up beautifully the feeling couples have that all they need is each other to be happy. Ask any married couple, however, and they will tell you that it is also important to learn about such mundane things as money management and budgeting if a marriage is going to succeed. Here are some money matters that you need to consider as you begin your marriage:

1. Credit. A good credit rating is a necessity in this world. Without it you cannot cash a check, buy a house, or even rent a car. To establish a good credit rating you must have a record of faithful, regular repayment of debt. Couples can begin to establish a combined credit rating by opening joint checking and savings accounts and by obtaining one of the many credit cards now available. The important thing in establishing credit is to pay your bills promptly and not to run up huge debts that you have no ability to repay. It is also important that you each maintain your individual credit rating. Thus, it might be helpful for each of you to have at least one credit card in your own name which you use occasionally and pay off immediately.

2. Debt. Many couples find that they can obtain credit easily—credit cards even come unsolicited through the mail! In the first few years of marriage, especially if they have two incomes, couples often find it tempting to purchase items on credit, enjoy them immediately, and pay for them later. If they accumulate too large a debt, however, couples can find themselves in serious financial trouble. If unexpected expenses occur, if one or both lose their jobs, if children arrive, the couple can quickly find themselves owing more money than they can repay. Sometimes they cannot even keep up the interest payments. If you find yourself in this situation, seek immediate financial counseling. An advisor can help you deal with creditors and arrange a repayment schedule that will allow you to maintain a good credit rating. Such a person can also teach you new spending and saving patterns as a couple.

3. Savings. Let's face it, most Americans do not save much money—especially when they are just starting out. There is no doubt, however, that it is important to save money if you want to own a home someday, send kids to college, or have a comfortable retirement. Even when you are just married, it is a good idea to get into the habit of trying to save some money. It may be advantageous, especially if you have two incomes, to save some money on a tax-deferred basis—either through a company pension plan or an individual retirement account. You should probably seek the advice of someone—parent, friend, accountant, banker—who can give you sound advice on these matters.

4. Insurance. Insurance is a protection against catastrophe. By pooling your premiums with those of millions of others, you share the risk with them of something terrible happening. Thus you need health, life, automobile, homeowners or renters, and perhaps disability insurance. It is important that you have sufficient coverage without becoming "insurance poor" by trying to protect yourself against every eventuality, no matter how remote. Find a good insurance agent you can trust and listen to the advice he or she gives, then together make up your own minds about how much insurance you need and can afford.

5. Wills. Most newly married people do not want to face the possibility that one or both of them might die suddenly or tragically. They therefore put off making their will until "later." That later often turns into "never" and often leaves a grieving widow or widower to deal with a complex set of legal and financial problems. Get a lawyer, draw up your wills, and be done with it. Then put the wills in a safe place that a trusted family member knows. While you are doing your wills, also consider drawing up "living wills" or "durable power of attorney" for medical decisions. These allow your loved ones to know what your wishes are regarding medical treatment in case you are unable to decide for yourself.

6. Budgets. As a means of coordinating resources and expenditures, a budget is a financial plan that allows a couple to manage income sensibly and ensure their financial security. A well-planned and well-executed budget can help free both of you from worries over money and avoid many unhappy arguments. Adopt a first-year budget to suit your special circumstances as a couple (see pages 60-61). Then see how it actually works out in practice and adapt it as you go along.

KNOWING THE TERRITORY

It is important for couples entering marriage to be totally aware of each other's present financial situation before making their financial arrangements as a couple. The wisest course is for each of you to lay out your financial picture as completely as possible before the wedding.

Be as honest as you can—this is no time for hiding the "bad news." Don't forget to include all possible liabilities, assets, and income. After you have each completed this exercise separately, exchange your sheets and discuss your financial situation openly and realistically.

YOUR LIABILITIES

	Monthly Payments (if applicable)	Total Still Owed (if applicable)	Payoff Date (if applicable)
1. Mortgage/Rent (including taxes)	$ _____	$ _____	_____
2. Car Loan	$ _____	$ _____	_____
3. Other Installment Loans	$ _____	$ _____	_____
4. Lines of Credit	$ _____	$ _____	_____
5. Credit Cards	$ _____	$ _____	_____
6. Other Loans	$ _____	$ _____	_____
A. Personal	$ _____	$ _____	_____
B. College	$ _____	$ _____	_____
C. Business	$ _____	$ _____	_____
7. Insurance	$ _____	$ _____	_____
A. Car	$ _____	$ _____	_____
B. Life	$ _____	$ _____	_____
C. Home	$ _____	$ _____	_____
D. Health/Disability (if not withheld)	$ _____	$ _____	_____
8. Income Taxes (if not withheld)	$ _____	$ _____	_____
9. Back Taxes Owed	$ _____	$ _____	_____
10. Medical and Dental Bills	$ _____	$ _____	_____
11. Pension/Retirement Contribution (if not withheld)	$ _____	$ _____	_____
12. Child Care	$ _____	$ _____	_____
13. Tuition/College Savings	$ _____	$ _____	_____
14. Child Support	$ _____	$ _____	_____
15. Alimony to Former Spouse	$ _____	$ _____	_____
16. Other:_____	$ _____	$ _____	_____
17. Other:_____	$ _____	$ _____	_____
TOTAL	$ _____	$ _____	_____

YOUR ASSETS

1. Real Estate $ _____
2. Cash Savings $ _____
3. Certificates of Deposit $ _____
4. Stocks and Bonds $ _____
5. Pension/Retirement Accounts $ _____
6. Cash Value LIfe Insurance $ _____
7. Other Investments $ _____
8. Cars $ _____
9. Furniture, Artwork, Jewelry $ _____
10. Expected Inheritance $ _____
11. Other Assets $ _____

Total $ _____

YOUR INCOME

1. Salary (take home) $ _____
2. Bonus $ _____
3. Dividends & Interest $ _____
4. Rental Income $ _____
5. Trusts and Gifts $ _____
6. Alimony $ _____
7. Child Support $ _____
8. Other Income $ _____

Total $ _____

A CLEAR PICTURE

Now that you have a clear picture of your financial situation, it's time to get down to the nitty-gritty, un-romantic task of financial planning. You may want to get some professional advice to help you plan your new family's financial future. Here are some immediate questions you should discuss:

Will there be enough money to cover your combined liabilities?

How can you best combine your assets?

What debts can be eliminated prior to the wedding?

How much will you be able to save from your combined incomes?

KNOWING THE TERRITORY

It is important for couples entering marriage to be totally aware of each other's present financial situation before making their financial arrangements as a couple. The wisest course is for each of you to lay out your financial picture as completely as possible before the wedding.

Be as honest as you can—this is no time for hiding the "bad news." Don't forget to include all possible liabilities, assets, and income. After you have each completed this exercise separately, exchange your sheets and discuss your financial situation openly and realistically.

YOUR LIABILITIES

	Monthly Payments (if applicable)	Total Still Owed (if applicable)	Payoff Date (if applicable)
1. Mortgage/Rent (including taxes)	$ _____	$ _____	_____
2. Car Loan	$ _____	$ _____	_____
3. Other Installment Loans	$ _____	$ _____	_____
4. Lines of Credit	$ _____	$ _____	_____
5. Credit Cards	$ _____	$ _____	_____
6. Other Loans	$ _____	$ _____	_____
A. Personal	$ _____	$ _____	_____
B. College	$ _____	$ _____	_____
C. Business	$ _____	$ _____	_____
7. Insurance	$ _____	$ _____	_____
A. Car	$ _____	$ _____	_____
B. Life	$ _____	$ _____	_____
C. Home	$ _____	$ _____	_____
D. Health/Disability (if not withheld)	$ _____	$ _____	_____
8. Income Taxes (if not withheld)	$ _____	$ _____	_____
9. Back Taxes Owed	$ _____	$ _____	_____
10. Medical and Dental Bills	$ _____	$ _____	_____
11. Pension/Retirement Contribution (if not withheld)	$ _____	$ _____	_____
12. Child Care	$ _____	$ _____	_____
13. Tuition/College Savings	$ _____	$ _____	_____
14. Child Support	$ _____	$ _____	_____
15. Alimony to Former Spouse	$ _____	$ _____	_____
16. Other:_____	$ _____	$ _____	_____
17. Other:_____	$ _____	$ _____	_____
TOTAL	$ _____	$ _____	_____

YOUR ASSETS

1. Real Estate $ _____
2. Cash Savings $ _____
3. Certificates of Deposit $ _____
4. Stocks and Bonds $ _____
5. Pension/Retirement Accounts $ _____
6. Cash Value LIfe Insurance $ _____
7. Other Investments $ _____
8. Cars $ _____
9. Furniture, Artwork, Jewelry $ _____
10. Expected Inheritance $ _____
11. Other Assets $ _____

Total $ _____

YOUR INCOME

1. Salary (take home) $ _____
2. Bonus $ _____
3. Dividends & Interest $ _____
4. Rental Income $ _____
5. Trusts and Gifts $ _____
6. Alimony $ _____
7. Child Support $ _____
8. Other Income $ _____

Total $ _____

A CLEAR PICTURE

Now that you have a clear picture of your financial situation, it's time to get down to the nitty-gritty, un-romantic task of financial planning. You may want to get some professional advice to help you plan your new family's financial future. Here are some immediate questions you should discuss:

Will there be enough money to cover your combined liabilities?

How can you best combine your assets?

What debts can be eliminated prior to the wedding?

How much will you be able to save from your combined incomes?

NUDEL

We invite you to play the NUDEL game, which should help you determine how closely you agree on the importance of the following items or services.

Consider each item, then make a check in the appropriate column.
- **N.** **N**ecessary
- **U.** very **U**seful
- **D.** merely **D**esirable, or
- **EL.** **E**xtra **L**uxury

	Necessary	Useful	Desirable	Extra Luxury
1. VCR/Cable TV				
2. Microwave				
3. Health insurance				
4. Pets				
5. Savings accounts				
6. Personal computer				
7. Sterling silverware/fine china				
8. Sports expenditures				
9. Extra bedroom in house or apartment				
10. Air conditioning				
11. Second car				
12. Stereo equipment				
13. Books and magazines				
14. Two incomes				
15. Fine furniture and art				
16. Health club membership				
17. Stocked liquor cabinet				
18. Vacations				
19. Stocks and bonds				
20. Credit cards				
21. Home ownership within five years				
22. Continuing education				
23. Tickets to cultural events				
24. Cellular phone				
25. Retirement savings				

YOUR FIRST YEAR BUDGET

MONTHS

INCOME	1	2	3	4	5	6	7	8	9	10	11	12	TOTAL
Salary(ies)													
Bonus(es)													
Dividends													
Interest													
Tax Returns													
Sale of Assets													
Other													
TOTAL INCOME													

MONTHS   ☐ ESTIMATED BUDGET   ▨ ACTUAL DOLLARS SPENT

	EXPENSES	1	2	3	4	5	6	7	8	9	10	11	12	TOTAL
HOUSING	Mortgage/Rent													
	Taxes													
	Insurance													
	Utilities													
	Maintenance													
	Improvement													
TRANSPORTATION	Car Payments													
	Insurance													
	Gas & Oil													
	Parking													
	License/Permits													
	Commuting													

Directions. Fill in your expense and income projections in the unshaded areas. As your year progresses, fill in the actual dollars spent and earned in the shaded areas. Compare those figures in the shaded areas to those in the unshaded areas to evaluate your budgeting. At the end we ask you to subtract expenses from income as a final measure of your financial situation. Good Luck! (Note: We've numbered the months rather than naming them as this is supposed to be a budget for your first year of marriage. You can start either with January or with your first month of marriage, whichever makes the most sense to you.)

MONTHS

	EXPENSES	1	2	3	4	5	6	7	8	9	10	11	12	TOTAL
Food	Groceries													
	Restaurants													
Clothing	Purchases													
	Cleaning													
Health Care	Medical/Dental													
	Drugs/Medicine													
	Insurance													
Recreation	Entertainment													
	Vacations													
	Hobbies													
	Gifts													
Other	Contributions													
	Life Insurance													
	Loan Payments													
	Savings													
	Personal Allow. HERS													
	Personal Allow. HIS													
	Miscellaneous													
	TOTAL EXPENSES													

12-MONTH SUMMARY

Estimated Income $ _____

LESS Estimated Expenses   – _____

Grand Total $ _____

12-MONTH SUMMARY

Actual Income $ _____

LESS Actual Expenses   – _____

Grand Total $ _____

NUDEL

We invite you to play the NUDEL game, which should help you determine how closely you agree on the importance of the following items or services.

Consider each item, then make a check in the appropriate column.
- **N.** **N**ecessary
- **U.** very **U**seful
- **D.** merely **D**esirable, or
- **EL.** **E**xtra **L**uxury

	Necessary	Useful	Desirable	Extra Luxury
1. VCR/Cable TV				
2. Microwave				
3. Health insurance				
4. Pets				
5. Savings accounts				
6. Personal computer				
7. Sterling silverware/fine china				
8. Sports expenditures				
9. Extra bedroom in house or apartment				
10. Air conditioning				
11. Second car				
12. Stereo equipment				
13. Books and magazines				
14. Two incomes				
15. Fine furniture and art				
16. Health club membership				
17. Stocked liquor cabinet				
18. Vacations				
19. Stocks and bonds				
20. Credit cards				
21. Home ownership within five years				
22. Continuing education				
23. Tickets to cultural events				
24. Cellular phone				
25. Retirement savings				

If the following question disturbs you, I am sorry. But as a marriage counselor with twenty-two years of experience, I am often asked, "What is the most common cause of marital break-ups?" In all honesty I have to answer . . . "Two people who should never have married in the first place—or, at least, should never have married each other."

Most of you will build satisfactory marriages; many of you will build very happy marriages. For the few of you who might not do either, the following warning signs might well indicate whether you should have second thoughts. I call them the fourteen "if's."

1 You may be very deeply in love, but if you have known each other for less than three months, professionals say it is doubtful that you have been acquainted long enough to really know the person you plan to marry. Better give yourselves and the relationship more time.

2 If your partner has been drunk or used drugs three times in the past three weeks or about ten times in the past three or four months, he or she may have a substance abuse problem. His or her dependency may require professional help. No marriage should begin if one partner is clearly unstable, troubled, or in need of professional help.

3 If your partner makes statements such as "I owe a great deal to mother. It's my duty to make her happy," and if such statements are coupled with behavior that makes it apparent that he or she will do almost anything to ensure parental approval, you should consider how close a relationship with in-laws a healthy marriage can sustain.

4 If you partner says things such as "I can't live without you; my life has no meaning apart from you; if I ever lost you I would kill myself," and if such statements are joined to very obvious dependent behavior, this partner may bring nothing to the relationship beyond deep draining needs. Being needed so desperately may flatter the ego for a while, but if that's all there is the relationship will become dull and draining.

5 If you have developed a pattern of quarreling with, disappointing, seriously irritating, or hurting each other during the majority of times that you have been together in the last three months, perhaps you are trying subconsciously to tell each other something. Think about it. Marriage will not erase this type of discontent.

6 If many of the significant, mature people in your life who love you—parents, relatives, teachers and especially good friends—indicate that you may be making a mistake, you should take pause. If people muster up the courage to comment (in words or otherwise) on another's decision in these private times we live in, weigh their opinions or nonverbal reactions carefully.

7 If some very serious problem or life transition occurred in the past few weeks, and if it is definitely troubling you, and if you have not had an opportunity to work it through, then either confront the problem or think about postponing the wedding.

8 If your financial situation is uncertain and there appears to be no means of correcting it in the near future, don't ignore it because "we're in love." Statistics show that financial problems are a significant factor in the breakup of at least 40% of all marriages. Although money cannot buy happiness, lack of financial stability can cause a great deal of stress and unhappiness.

63

9 If all of your friends are marrying and you feel pressured to do the same, don't! You can sustain any amount of societal or peer pressure to avoid an unhappy life. If you feel like it's time in your life to get married, or that your current state in life is unsatisfying and you're thinking marriage might be the answer, think again! If you want to marry because you're afraid you are moving beyond "marrying age" or "child rearing years," don't. Getting married just to satisfy some "biological clock" will not work.

10 If both of you are 18 years of age or under, your potential for divorce is 3-1/2 times greater than that of other people who are 21 years of age and over.

11 If you are marrying because you just have to get out of the house, you will ultimately hurt only yourself if marriage is merely a means of asserting your freedom or "getting back" at your parents for past hurts. Moving out of the house might be very appropriate, but should marriage be the excuse or the way?

12 If you feel that having become sexually involved commits you to marrying each other despite serious problems in your relationship, don't. A good marriage is predicated on maturity and responsibility, not on sexual involvement which may not be founded on love.

13 If you are a pregnant couple (it does take two!), then slow down, think, talk, ponder, and pray. Neither pregnancy itself nor the fear of any social stigma that pregnancy might cause is a good reason to marry. Ask yourselves whether you would really marry one another if there were no pregnancy.

14 If your ethnic or cultural backgrounds differ so greatly that conflicts over important matters have already occurred, the difficulties will likely increase when you marry. How do you honor each other's backgrounds? Have you developed effective ways to talk through the differences?

15 In an argument or conflict, if one partner always compromises and the other never does, beware that anger and resentment will build until one day it will explode, perhaps causing permanent damage to your relationship. If this is your pattern, talk about it now and see if you *both* can change.

SECOND THOUGHTS?

No one can predict that your marriage will fail or succeed, and none of these warning signs spell absolute disaster. The risk that you take is part of the adventure of marriage. But, if you decide to take that risk, you must first consider the odds. Are they in your favor? If not, *you might* be taking a far greater risk than you should.

Please do not panic, bury your head in the sand, or hit the road. But, do think it over and talk it over. Make certain that you are acting responsibly in that your decision to marry is made with good judgment. You might want to ask advice from a qualified, unbiased person, such as a member of the clergy, or a married person.

Although marriage is wonderful, it is also a life-long task that should be given careful consideration before a lasting decision is made or binding action taken. You owe it to one another to be honest about your feelings and your situation. *Only* good *can come of it.*

The more open and honest you and your partner are about your feelings and attitudes toward sex, the more fulfilling your overall relationship will be. Granted, sex is not the easiest subject to discuss openly—primarily because almost everyone experiences some anxiety when trying to verbalize feelings about sex. Although a natural aspect of human nature, sex is not simple; it involves roles, gender, physiology, emotions, and even a bit of mystery. No one has all the right answers, so you need not be experienced to be able to discuss sex—just open to discussion and willing to listen.

To engage in open dialogue about sex, you must first understand yourself as a sexual being: What has influenced you? How do you feel about sex? How do you feel about your partner sexually?

The questions in this exercise are designed to assist you in an honest appraisal of your sexual self. Jot down your responses and share them with your partner. Then listen to each other.

1. Do you think that sex is fun, frightening, threatening, satisfying, holy, expressive of your relationship, other? Give two descriptions that characterize your feelings about sex. _____

_____

_____

_____

_____

_____

2. How do you express affection? _____

_____

_____

_____

3. How do you express your need for affection?

_____

_____

_____

4. How do you feel about your body? _____

_____

_____

_____

5. What events and attitudes from your past—especially any previous relationships—have influenced your sexual behaviors and attitudes?

_____

_____

_____

6. What memories or hang-ups (if any) must you work through to become comfortable and confident with your sexuality? _____

_____

_____

_____

7. Once married, who do you expect will be the one to initiate lovemaking? _____

_____

_____

_____

8. Under what circumstances will you say "no" to making love? How will you feel when your beloved says "no"? _____

_____

_____

_____

9. As a sexual partner, a woman should _____

_____

_____

_____

10. As a sexual partner, a man should _____

_____

_____

_____

11. What circumstances do you find most exciting sexually? _____

_____

_____

_____

12. When would you not want to have sex? ___

_____

_____

_____

13. Do you find any specific acts immoral (improper) in marriage? Do you have any hesitations or reservations about sex? _____

_____

_____

_____

14. Are you aware of the risk of AIDS from sex? Have the two of you discussed AIDS? Have either of you been tested for the AIDS virus? __

_____

_____

_____

15. Have the two of you talked about family planning? What have you decided? Who made the decision?_____

_____

_____

_____

16. What do you find physically attractive about your future spouse? _____

_____

_____

_____

17. What do you think your future spouse finds physically attractive about you? _____

_____

_____

_____

18. If your sex life was in trouble, would you seek counseling? Would your partner agree to it? ___

_____

_____

_____

19. What other sexual feeling, thought, or concern do you want your future spouse know? ___

_____

_____

_____

20. What are your hopes for your lovemaking? _

_____

_____

_____

The more open and honest you and your partner are about your feelings and attitudes toward sex, the more fulfilling your overall relationship will be. Granted, sex is not the easiest subject to discuss openly—primarily because almost everyone experiences some anxiety when trying to verbalize feelings about sex. Although a natural aspect of human nature, sex is not simple; it involves roles, gender, physiology, emotions, and even a bit of mystery. No one has all the right answers, so you need not be experienced to be able to discuss sex—just open to discussion and willing to listen.

To engage in open dialogue about sex, you must first understand yourself as a sexual being: What has influenced you? How do you feel about sex? How do you feel about your partner sexually?

The questions in this exercise are designed to assist you in an honest appraisal of your sexual self. Jot down your responses and share them with your partner. Then listen to each other.

1. Do you think that sex is fun, frightening, threatening, satisfying, holy, expressive of your relationship, other? Give two descriptions that characterize your feelings about sex. _____

_____

_____

_____

_____

_____

2. How do you express affection? _____

_____

_____

_____

3. How do you express your need for affection?

_____

_____

_____

4. How do you feel about your body? _____

_____

_____

_____

5. What events and attitudes from your past—especially any previous relationships—have influenced your sexual behaviors and attitudes?

_____

_____

_____

6. What memories or hang-ups (if any) must you work through to become comfortable and confident with your sexuality? _____

_____

_____

_____

7. Once married, who do you expect will be the one to initiate lovemaking? _____

_____

_____

8. Under what circumstances will you say "no" to making love? How will you feel when your beloved says "no"? _____

_____

_____

_____

9. As a sexual partner, a woman should _____

_____

_____

_____

10. As a sexual partner, a man should _____

_____

_____

_____

11. What circumstances do you find most exciting sexually? _____

_____

_____

_____

12. When would you not want to have sex? ___

_____

_____

_____

13. Do you find any specific acts immoral (improper) in marriage? Do you have any hesitations or reservations about sex? _____

_____

_____

_____

14. Are you aware of the risk of AIDS from sex? Have the two of you discussed AIDS? Have either of you been tested for the AIDS virus? __

_____

_____

_____

15. Have the two of you talked about family planning? What have you decided? Who made the decision? _____

_____

_____

_____

16. What do you find physically attractive about your future spouse? _____

_____

_____

_____

17. What do you think your future spouse finds physically attractive about you? _____

_____

_____

_____

18. If your sex life was in trouble, would you seek counseling? Would your partner agree to it? ___

_____

_____

_____

19. What other sexual feeling, thought, or concern do you want your future spouse know? ___

_____

_____

_____

20. What are your hopes for your lovemaking? _

_____

_____

OUR FAVORITE THINGS

In any conversation—especially with a loved one—it is assumed that when one person speaks the other is listening. Spouses in successful marriages learn to listen to each other with their ears, their eyes, their sense of touch. They are as aware of their partner's feelings as of what is said. They try to give all of their physical, psychological, and emotional attention to the other. Listening is critical to effective communication in marriage.

This exercise will help you understand how well you listen to your partner. If you have listened well over these months or years that you have known each other, you certainly should be able to list each other's ten favorite things to do. Here's the test!

Working alone, list the ten things you most enjoy doing. Then list the ten things you think your partner will put on his or her list. When you are finished, share your responses with each other. Where you or your partner have guessed wrong about the other's interests, talk about why one or both of you had not "heard" well before.

_____

MY FAVORITE THINGS

1. _____

2. _____

3. _____

4. _____

5. _____

6. _____

7. _____

8. _____

9. _____

10. _____

YOUR FAVORITE THINGS

1. _____

2. _____

3. _____

4. _____

5. _____

6. _____

7. _____

8. _____

9. _____

10. _____

READ THE FUTURE

Although no one can accurately predict the future, couples who are able to look ahead, project their hopes and desires, and speculate on the possibilities that their life together holds, are usually far more realistic. They are more flexible and better able to adapt to unusual events than those for whom every new experience is a shock or surprise.

Engage your imaginations—dream a little about the various stages of your marriage—and jot down short sentences or phrases that describe some of the features of your marriage as it might be in the second, seventh, fifteenth, and twenty-fifth years. For each stage of married life indicated below, try to describe your life together as it might relate to **children, career changes, family income, religious involvement,** and **changing goals.** Compare your projections and discuss them.

2nd Year

7th Year

15th Year

25th Year

OUR FAVORITE THINGS

In any conversation—especially with a loved one—it is assumed that when one person speaks the other is listening. Spouses in successful marriages learn to listen to each other with their ears, their eyes, their sense of touch. They are as aware of their partner's feelings as of what is said. They try to give all of their physical, psychological, and emotional attention to the other. Listening is critical to effective communication in marriage.

This exercise will help you understand how well you listen to your partner. If you have listened well over these months or years that you have known each other, you certainly should be able to list each other's ten favorite things to do. Here's the test!

Working alone, list the ten things you most enjoy doing. Then list the ten things you think your partner will put on his or her list. When you are finished, share your responses with each other. Where you or your partner have guessed wrong about the other's interests, talk about why one or both of you had not "heard" well before.

MY FAVORITE THINGS

1. _____
2. _____
3. _____
4. _____
5. _____
6. _____
7. _____
8. _____
9. _____
10. _____

YOUR FAVORITE THINGS

1. _____
2. _____
3. _____
4. _____
5. _____
6. _____
7. _____
8. _____
9. _____
10. _____

READ THE FUTURE

Although no one can accurately predict the future, couples who are able to look ahead, project their hopes and desires, and speculate on the possibilities that their life together holds, are usually far more realistic. They are more flexible and better able to adapt to unusual events than those for whom every new experience is a shock or surprise.

Engage your imaginations—dream a little about the various stages of your marriage—and jot down short sentences or phrases that describe some of the features of your marriage as it might be in the second, seventh, fifteenth, and twenty-fifth years. For each stage of married life indicated below, try to describe your life together as it might relate to **children, career changes, family income, religious involvement,** and **changing goals.** Compare your projections and discuss them.

2nd Year

7th Year

15th Year

25th Year

Because of a divorce, the death of a spouse, or the annulment of a previous marriage, many people today are either getting married again, marrying someone who has been married before, or both. It is extremely important to recognize that any previous marriage will have an impact on your current relationship. If one or both of you have been married before, then *both* should do this exercise.

Working separately, write your responses to the questions below. (If a statement does not apply to you, simply skip it.) Then come together and share your answers, being especially sensitive to the feelings of the other person and open with your own. If there are any children involved on either side, then do the same with the questions on the next page.

---

1. I am convinced that our marriage is not being done on the "rebound" from a prior marriage because _____

_____

_____

_____

2. One thing from a prior marriage that might cause tension in our relationship is _____

_____

_____

_____

3. The following issues from a prior marriage will be the most challenging for us (check all that apply):

___ contact with a former spouse

___ contact with former in-laws

___ child visitation

___ finances

___ other (name each):

_____

_____

_____

4. On occasion, certain situations trigger responses that seem connected to a prior marriage and have no place in our relationship. A recent example was _____

_____

_____

5. Even though we've talked about where we'll be living after the wedding, I'm still concerned that

_____

_____

_____

6. My or my partner's experience with money in a prior marriage shouldn't affect us now, but ___

_____

_____

_____

7. I hope that experience in a prior marriage won't cause us problems with religion or spirituality, such as _____

_____

_____

(STEP) FATHERING

Many marriages begin with one or more children already on the scene from a previous marriage or marriages. This raises special issues of parenting and successfully blending the child or children into a new family unit.

Working separately, answer each of the questions below. Then share your responses with your partner, looking especially for areas where you have given greatly different answers.

A. List three things you think you both agree upon in your approach to parenting.

1. _____
2. _____
3. _____

B. What are your three greatest concerns about having a blended family?

1. _____
2. _____
3. _____

C. What are the three qualities that will make you a good father or stepfather?

1. _____
2. _____
3. _____

D. What are the three qualities that will make your future wife a good mother or stepmother?

1. _____
2. _____
3. _____

E. What do you want/expect the children to call you?

1. Your own children from a previous marriage:

_____

2. Your future wife's children from a previous marriage:

_____

3. Any children you might have together:

_____

F. What do you want/expect the children to call your future wife?

1. Her own children from a previous marriage:

_____

2. Your children from a previous marriage:

_____

3. Any children you might have together:

_____

G. If there are non-custodial children involved, what are three practical concerns that will have to be addressed immediately?

1. _____
2. _____
3. _____

REMARRIAGE

Because of a divorce, the death of a spouse, or the annulment of a previous marriage, many people today are either getting married again, marrying someone who has been married before, or both. It is extremely important to recognize that any previous marriage will have an impact on your current relationship. If one or both of you have been married before, then *both* should do this exercise.

Working separately, write your responses to the questions below. (If a statement does not apply to you, simply skip it.) Then come together and share your answers, being especially sensitive to the feelings of the other person and open with your own. If there are any children involved on either side, then do the same with the questions on the next page.

---

1. I am convinced that our marriage is not being done on the "rebound" from a prior marriage because _____

_____

_____

_____

2. One thing from a prior marriage that might cause tension in our relationship is _____

_____

_____

_____

3. The following issues from a prior marriage will be the most challenging for us (check all that apply):

___ contact with a former spouse

___ contact with former in-laws

___ child visitation

___ finances

___ other (name each):

_____

_____

_____

4. On occasion, certain situations trigger responses that seem connected to a prior marriage and have no place in our relationship. A recent example was _____

_____

_____

5. Even though we've talked about where we'll be living after the wedding, I'm still concerned that

_____

_____

_____

6. My or my partner's experience with money in a prior marriage shouldn't affect us now, but ___

_____

_____

_____

7. I hope that experience in a prior marriage won't cause us problems with religion or spirituality, such as _____

_____

_____

(STEP) MOTHERING

Many marriages begin with one or more children already on the scene from a previous marriage or marriages. This raises special issues of parenting and successfully blending the child or children into a new family unit.

Working separately, answer each of the questions below. Then share your responses with your partner, looking especially for areas where you have given greatly different answers.

A. List three things you think you both agree upon in your approach to parenting.

1. _____
2. _____
3. _____

B. What are your three greatest concerns about having a blended family?

1. _____
2. _____
3. _____

C. What are the three qualities that will make you a good mother or stepmother?

1. _____
2. _____
3. _____

D. What are the three qualities that will make your future husband a good father or stepfather?

1. _____
2. _____
3. _____

E. What do you want/expect the children to call you?

1. Your own children from a previous marriage:

_____

2. Your future husband's children from a previous marriage:

_____

3. Any children you might have together:

_____

F. What do you want/expect the children to call your future husband?

1. His own children from a previous marriage:

_____

2. Your children from a previous marriage:

_____

3. Any children you might have together:

_____

G. If there are non-custodial children involved, what are three practical concerns that will have to be addressed immediately?

1. _____
2. _____
3. _____

Cohabitation (couples living together before marriage) is one of the most sensitive and volatile areas in marriage preparation. The *Catechism of the Catholic Church* states that "Human love does not tolerate 'trial marriages.' It demands a total and definitive gift of persons to one another." Statements by many different religious bodies explore the moral and pastoral implications of this issue in greater detail. You should speak with the clergy or lay people helping you prepare for marriage if you are living together or thinking about doing so before marriage.

Consider together the following questions and statements. When you have finished discussing them, decide together openly and honestly how the two of you are going to deal with the issue of cohabitation for the time remaining before your marriage.

1 If you are already living together, why did you begin? For example, were either of you afraid of making a permanent commitment? Did you want to "test out" your relationship? Was it a matter of convenience or need for companionship or financial savings? Did one or both of you need to escape from a bad home situation? Discuss whether these conditions or considerations still exist.

2 How has your relationship changed over the time you have known each other? What have you learned about yourselves and each other from the experience? How might your views have been influenced by living together?

3 To you, what are the major differences between living together and entering into a Christian marriage?

4 Some couples who cohabit tend to refrain from discussing troublesome issues in their relationship because they might cause immediate practical problems. Are there any problems—large or small—that the two of you have been avoiding because you didn't want to "rock the boat"? Discuss them now.

5 Some cohabiting couples choose to marry at a time when one or the other partner delivers an ultimatum, such as "Either we marry now or we go our separate ways." Has anything like that occurred in your relationship? Discuss whether either one of you feel pressured to marry now.

6 Couples who live together before marriage may think that their lives will not change much after the wedding, yet experience shows otherwise. Some relationships actually become more stormy after marriage simply because one or both partners may feel more secure and bring up issues that were ignored or repressed while living together. Other relationships lose some of their intensity once the "honeymoon" is over. Discuss whether either of you worries about how your relationship might change after marriage.

7 Living apart before marriage allows a couple the physical and psychological space they need to be more objective about their relationship and freer about their commitment. Discuss this idea.

8 What are each of your reasons for becoming married now?

DOMESTIC ABUSE

Some couples find themselves in a marriage that is wonderful one day and terrible the next. Even though at times they can experience great joy in their love, they know that something is wrong with the relationship. What may be occurring are sometimes subtle, but very real, forms of physical, psychological or verbal abuse.

Domestic abuse is commonly described as a pattern of learned behavior in which one person uses force or manipulation to control another. This behavior can occur rarely, or it can be a daily event.

Physical abuse can range from hitting, pushing, shoving, etc. to criminal assault, sexual abuse (unwanted, forced sexual activity), and stalking. Other forms of abuse—excessive yelling, belittling or undermining the other's self esteem, the "silent treatment" or other "game playing," lying or twisting the truth, taunting, threatening, financial manipulation, destruction of property, etc.—may not be criminal but can be just as damaging.

Domestic abuse occurs among all economic, educational, ethnic, racial and religious groups, but it is never an acceptable means of self-expression or problem-solving for a loving couple. Each human being is a good, valued, beloved child of God who is entitled to a safe and healthy environment. Abuse of any kind can make a person a terrorized victim in his or her own home.

Think carefully about this description of domestic abuse. Does anything ring a bell or send up a warning flag regarding your relationship? Even if neither of you have ever physically harmed the other, you may have exhibited other forms of abusive behavior with each other. (Excessive use of alcohol or drugs often accompanies domestic abuse.)

Such activities are almost always shrouded in secrecy. Even your family or closest friends may not know that they are occurring in your relationship. Abuse, however tame or severe, cannot survive in the open. Here are a couple of signs that domestic abuse may be something you need to worry about:

1. Are there negative or troubling patterns of activity between the two of you of which nobody else is aware and you feel obligated to keep secret?

2. Do you feel in any way put down or isolated in your relationship?

If you answer yes to either of these questions, it is an indication that domestic abuse may be a damaging factor in your relationship, and you must do something about it *now*. If you think things will change once your are married, you are wrong. The only change that is likely is that the abusive behavior will escalate in its frequency, intensity and seriousness.

Here is what to do if you suspect that you are being abused:

1. Believe in yourself. Know that you are not to blame for another's behavior. Remember that you are created in God's very image and likeness, that you deserve respect, that you can make changes, and that you are not alone.

2. Break the cycle of secrecy. Take the risk to talk to a trusted friend, counselor, or minister. Tell that person what troubles you and describe the abusive behavior. He or she will likely have an objective view and be able to tell you if you should be concerned or not. This person will also become your ally and supporter if further action is needed.

3. Call off or postpone the wedding. Yes, this is a drastic step that will surely cause some embarrassment and may even lead to rethinking your marriage, but if there is any indication of serious abuse in your relationship, *it is not the time to get married!*

4. **Pray**. God will surely give you the strength to do what you fear to do but know you must do.

If you think you might be in an abusive situation, you can call the following:

National Council on Family Violence
Hotline: 800-222-2000

Local religious or social services agencies, such as Catholic Charities or Lutheran Social Services, whose telephone numbers can be found in the yellow or blue pages of phone books under "Social Service Agencies."

In an emergency or life-threatening situation, call the police.
